ENCOUNTERS

by
Rabbi Aryeh Kaplan

MOZNAIM PUBLISHING CORPORATION
NEW YORK / JERUSALEM

Copyright © 1990 by Moznaim Publishing Corporation

All rights reserved. This book, or parts thereof, may not be reproduced in any form without the written permission of the publisher.

For information write:
Moznaim Publishing Corporation
4304 12th Avenue
Brooklyn, New York 11219
Tel. (718) 438-7680, 853-0525

Printed and bound in Jerusalem, Israel
by Vagshal Ltd.
Typesetting by Vagshal Ltd.
Jerusalem

Printed in Israel

This book
is dedicated to the memory of
RABBI ARYEH KAPLAN ז״ל
from his children and grandchildren,
The Kaplan and Rosenfeld Families.

TABLE OF CONTENTS

Introduction 7

PART I: Man and G-d

1. Meet the Real You 13
2. Preparing for Eternity 18
3. Why Am I Living? 25
4. Meet Your Creator 29
5. Prayer 36
6. How Man Created G-d 43
7. Wanted: G-d Dead or Alive 48
8. Knowing and Remembering 51

PART II: The Jew and Society

1. Why is a Jew? 63
2. Three Truths 67
3. Let Not Guilt Be Your Ruin 72
4. Taking Time Out 79
5. Dust From the Earth 86
6. The Call of the Shofar 91
7. A City Without Walls 97
8. Is Judaism Worth Saving? 103
9. War Resistance in Jewish Law 109
10. The Generation Gap 118
11. The End of Death 121
12. When Bones Rise Again 125

INTRODUCTION

by Rabbi Pinchas Stolper

Who else but Rabbi Aryeh Kaplan possessed the magic touch with which to make complicated and mysterious philosophical religious concepts come to life with clarity, simplicity and force. Only he was able to lower his pail deep into the wellsprings of our tradition, deeper than had been done in English until his time, and bring us cool, refreshing and revealing Torah insights.

Aryeh Kaplan lives on through the writings he left behind — a living legacy of piercing and penetrating thought.

Religious concepts are often difficult, and seemingly unreachable. Rabbi Kaplan brings them into focus. He had the rare ability to connect science to Torah, philosophy to action, mysticism to clarity of thought. He knew how to take abstract concepts and give them life. He had the talent to restore faith, to bring G-d's living message to our hearts and minds. Despite the fact that he was a deep and distinguished scholar, a talmid chacham who had mastered all branches of the Torah, he possessed the common touch; he understood how people think and had the ability to translate deep and complicated concepts into everyday language.

Rabbi Aryeh Kaplan's meteoric rise as one of the most effective, persuasive, scholarly and prolific exponents of Judaism in the English language came to an abrupt end on January 28, 1983, with his sudden death at the age of 48. Rabbi Kaplan was a multi-faceted, uniquely creative and talented author, scholar, thinker, rabbi and educator who touched the lives of thousands. The 47 volumes that were his life's work accounted for a qualitative and quantitative leap in Jewish publishing, making a host of difficult topics and concepts available to the English-reading public.

In the course of a writing career spanning only 12 years, Aryeh Kaplan became known to Jewish youth and adult readers for such books as *Waters of Eden — The Mystery of the Mikvah; Sabbath — Day of Eternity; G-d, Man and Tefilin; Tzizit — The Thread of Light; The Light Beyond; Adventure in Chassidic Thought (An Anthology); The Handbook of Jewish Thought; The Bahir — A Commentary and Translation; Meditation and the Bible; Meditation and the Kaballah; Jewish Meditation;* and *Made in Heaven — A Jewish Wedding Guide.*

Rabbi Kaplan was a resourceful and creative translator, as his translation of the Five Books of Moses, *The Living Torah*, attests.

Rabbi Kaplan was born in New York City and was educated in the Torah Vodaath and Mir Yeshivos in Brooklyn. After years of study at Jerusalem's Mir Yeshiva, he was ordained by some of Israel's foremost rabbinic authorities. He also earned a Master's degree in physics and was listed in *Who's Who in Physics* in the United States. "I use my physics background to analyze and systemize data, very much like a physicist would deal with physical reality," Rabbi Kaplan once said.

I first encountered this extraordinary individual when I spotted his article on "Immortality in the Soul" and was taken by his unusual ability to explain a difficult topic — one usually reserved for advanced scholars and almost completely untouched previously in English — so simply it could be understood by any intelligent reader. It was clear that this special ability could fill a significant void in English Judaica.

When I invited Rabbi Kaplan to write on the concept of tefillin for the Orthodox Union's National Conference of Synagogue Youth, he completed the 96 page *G-d, Man and Tefillin* — with sources and footnotes from the Talmud, Midrash and *Zohar* — in less than 2 weeks. The book — masterful, comprehensive, inspiring yet simple — set a pattern which was to characterize all of his succeeding works.

A soft-spoken, unassuming individual, modest despite his spreading renown and popularity, Aryeh Kaplan was an activist, a firm believer in acquainting unaffiliated and alienated Jewish youth with their heritage. He was a prime force behind the teshuvah movement, the return to Jewish observance. "Throughout history, Jews have always been observant," he noted in an interview. "The teshuvah movement is just a normalization. The Jewish people are sort of getting their act back together again. We are just doing what we are supposed to be doing." Indeed, his books reflect a similar, upbeat philosophy. The message he tried to get across was that "Judaism is a live, growing concern. A person looking for meaning in life need not go anywhere else."

Aryeh Kaplan's unusual warmth, sincerity and total dedication to Torah were an inspiration to the thousands he reached personally. His home was always open, his table crowded with Sabbath guests and students. He traveled far and wide to share his knowledge and commitment with young people at seminars, retreats and college campuses.

Rabbi Aryeh Moshe Eliyahu ben Shmuel Kaplan abandoned a promising career in physics, deciding instead to devote himself totally to the dissemination of Torah. He succeeded in uniting many elements in one personality — he was the Talmudic sage, the man of Halachah, the master of Western civilization, and the scientist, with an uncanny grasp of Kaballah, Jewish mysticism and Chassidic thought.

In the process of bringing Torah to the masses, Rabbi Kaplan revealed much of which was previously hidden. His mind contained libraries of books, waiting to be put into writing. It was the will of the L-rd that so much be revealed and no more.

PART ONE

MAN AND G-D

MEET THE REAL YOU

Solomon, the wisest of all men, asked, "Who knows the spirit of man, whether it goes upward, and the spirit of the beast, whether it goes downward to the earth?" (Ecclesiastes 3:21). What is this spirit of man? Is it distinct from the person? If so, what is a person? Can we begin to discuss the fate of this spirit before we know what it is, before we know what man is? Can we consider our future without defining what we are now? Before thinking about your spirit, I must ask you to think about yourself. What are you really? Who is the real you?

Before we examine these deep and abstract questions, let's look at the concrete and evident aspects of a person. Take your hand, for example. Look at it. Think about it. What do you see? It is a part of your body, a limb, an appendage, made of bone and sinew and covered with flesh and skin. It is filled with nerves and blood vessels. There are lymph ducts running through it, connecting it to your body, making it part of you.

Look at your hand. It opens and closes; it obeys every command that your mind sends it. It is yours — it is part of you.

But what are you? What happens when you tell your hand to open and close? How does your mind will your hand to open? Who is telling your hand to close?

Now, let's consider the whole person. Point to yourself. If you are like most people, you will point your finger at your chest, at your heart, at your body. But is your body really you? Not too long ago, a person could consider his body an integral part of himself. You were your body and your body was you. But this is no longer the case. Scientific progress has changed the entire concept of human identity.

This new era was born in the late 1960's, when a hopeful and awestruck world witnessed one man's dramatic struggle for life. Dr. Philip Blaiburg lived for a year and a half with someone else's heart beating in his breast. If I had asked Dr. Blaiburg to point to himself, would he have pointed to his chest? Was this heart, transplanted from another human being, really part of him?

Dr. Blaiburg once described his emotions when he saw his own, that is, his original, heart suspended in a jar of formaldehyde. How does a man feel, holding his own heart in his hands? Which heart was really Dr. Blaiburg's? Now, ask yourself, is the heart that beats inside you, the one you pointed at, is this the real you? Or are you something else entirely?

In 1969, the idea of transplanting a human heart, alive and beating, into another person seemed like a miracle. Today, it is almost commonplace. Today, the advances of science are even more radical. Researchers predict things that will force us to change our way of thinking completely.

One of the things that researchers are predicting, perhaps within the next decade or two, is a brain transplant. A living brain could be taken from one human body and placed in another. Such a feat would force us to face this question: Just what is the human personality?

Imagine that you have an incurable disease in your body, but that your brain remains healthy. The doctors find a donor for you — a person who has irreparable brain damage, whose brain has ceased to function, but whose body is healthy. You are placed under anesthesia. Your brain is removed from your present body — the body too sick to sustain life — and is placed in this new, healthy body. Now, imagine that you wake up. You still have your old brain, with all your memories. Your complete personality has remained intact, with all your old behavior patterns; your original thinking patterns are still functioning. But now you have a brand-new body: new hands, new feet, new eyes, new ears, and a new heart. Your original body was old and sick, wasting away, but now you have a young new body, healthy and full of energy.

Now if I asked you to point to yourself, would you point to your chest, to your body? Remember, you have your old brain, your old thoughts, your old memories, but a new body. Who is the real you? Is it that old body, lying lifeless on a slab? Or is it this new one, the body that you can now control with your thoughts? Is this *your* body at all? Perhaps the real you is your brain. As our knowlege progresses, the questions become more and more complex, and we must search further still.

We live in the age of computers. The technological advances are too rapid for the layman to follow. Each generation of computers is more sophisticated than the previous one — the supercomputers outperform their predecessors many thousands of times over. Each generation is more complex, faster and literally more intelligent. Much of the advanced computer technology is developed through the science of cybernetics. This science draws comparisons between advanced computers and the human brain. In many ways, extremely complex computers behave much like the human brain, and to a large extent, the human brain behaves like an extremely complex computer. Through cybernetics, computer engineers use our knowledge of the human brain to design better computers, and psychologists are able to use our knowledge of computers to gain greater insights into the workings of the human brain.

In computer technology, it is possible to program a memory transfer. That is, all the information in one computer can be transferred to another. This takes place electronically; all that passes from one computer to the other is information, data carried by electrical impulse. Cyberneticists have speculated whether it would be possible to do the same with the human brain. This concept is a favorite theme of science fiction writers.

But many serious scientists believe that it would be possible. And even if it is not possible in practice, it is possible in theory.

Let us try to envision a human memory transfer. A person has an incurable disease; neither his body nor his brain can be salvaged. We grow a new human body, brain and all, a genetic clone of the original, in some kind of chemical nutrient solution. This is not possible now, but advances in bioengineering suggest that it might be possible in a decade or two. So a new body is grown — a new body with a blank brain. The new brain is capable of functioning, but it lacks memories and thought patterns. It has never been used at all. We now take the final step: we perform a memory transfer from the sick person to the new brain lodged in the new body.

Now we must deal with a fascinating concept. If all of a person's memories, thought patterns, and personality traits could be transferred to a new body and brain, that person would literally exist in the new body, in the new brain, even though nothing physical has changed, even though no physical part of him has been transplanted to the new body. All that has been transferred, all that has been placed in the new body, is a certain amount of data, information that up until now existed in the old brain. This "information" contains the sum total of this person's personality.

All this is possible, at least in theory. Now, ask again, who is the real you? It can't be your body, nor even your brain. It can only be the "information" contained in your brain: your memories, your personality, and your thought patterns.

What, then, happens when no brain transplant or memory transfer takes place, when a person's original body deteriorates and dies? What happens to all his "information"? After the brain becomes inert and the body decays, what happens to the "data bank" that seems, in our deeper analysis, to be the real person? When a book is burned, its contents are destroyed. When a computer is smashed, or even unplugged, its information is permanently erased. When a person dies, does the same thing happen? Is the mind — the personality, the thought patterns and memories — irretrievably lost?

We know that G-d is omniscient. He knows everything and remembers everything — every thought, every memory, every personality trait of every human being. He is aware of every single thing that exists within our minds. So when a person dies, does G-d forget it all? Certainly not! Even after a person's death, all of this "information" remains and continues to exist in G-d's memory.

We may think of something that exists "in memory" alone as being static — fixed pieces of data, lifeless facts. But G-d's thoughts and memory are not static. The sum total of a human personality may indeed exist in G-d's memory, but this is not the same as existing in human memory. In G-d's memory, the human personality can still maintain its identity. It can still maintain its volition and it can remain active. This is what we call the human soul. This is what lives on, even after a person dies.

It is very difficult for us to imagine an active personality, a living entity, existing within G-d's memory. The entire concept of G-d's mind is most difficult to comprehend. So we give it names that we can grasp. We say that a soul is in Heaven, or in Paradise. We describe the soul as dwelling in the World to Come, in the World of Souls. We say that it rests in the "bond of eternal life."

The Kabbalists describe the soul as a *chelek Eloka mi-m'al* — a portion of G-d Himself, from above. And Scripture is quite explicit about the destiny of that soul: "The dust returns to the earth as it was, but the spirit returns to G-d Who gave it" (Ecclesiastes 12:7). This is meant quite literally. The body, even the physical brain, which can at least in theory be discarded or exchanged, returns to the dust of the earth, but the personality, the soul, lives on in G-d's memory, in G-d's eternal thought. This soul, which will forever maintain its identity, is the essential person. This is the real you.

PREPARING FOR ETERNITY

> G-d will redeem my soul from the power of the grave,
> For He will receive me indeed. (Psalms 49:16)

A famous psychologist once noted that young children imagine that they will live forever. Then, one day, the child makes a horrible discovery. Someone he knows, a neighbor or a relative, passes away, and the child is shocked into reality: life comes to an end. Slowly, it dawns on the child that what happened to others will happen to him; someday he too will die. And as his fantasy of immortality fades, a bit of childhood innocence vanishes forever.

Soon, the fearful shock gives way to questions, to wonder. What is it like to die? What is death really like? What will happen to me?

The child grows and matures and learns to stifle his questions. They don't seem so urgent as he perceives how slowly time passes. They don't bother him so acutely, at least not now. But this childish wonder, born of the fearful shock, the first knowledge of death, remains buried within him. Indeed, it remains deep within all of us. And we worry, what is it like to pass through the gates of death? And even more important, what will we experience when our time comes?

There are some who deny that Judaism has any answers to such questions. They say that Judaism teaches us to live a good life in this world and not to worry about the next. This is true — and not true. While Judaism directs our energies toward the life we know, it does not stifle our worries; it frees us from them. It is true: life is important and man's life in this world is sacred. But man's destiny does not end with this life. The great classics of Judaism — the Talmud, the Midrash, the philosophical works and major codes — all ponder the ultimate question of death and immortality. Their conclusions are fundamental to the teachings of Judaism, permeating the entire structure of Jewish theology.

> G-d will redeem my soul from the power of the grave,
> For He will receive me indeed.

What is this power of the grave? And what does the Psalmist mean, to be received by G-d? Despite our show of worldly sophistication, we are all burdened by such questions. But, if we wish to be faithful to the Jewish ideal, if we truly believe in the sanctity of life, then we must first address another question: What is it like to live? Before we explore the phenomenon of death, we must first take a careful look at the phenomenon of life.

Life begins at conception. Two microscopic germs unite and become one; a new man has begun. His existence unfolds as an atom of life, a living atom containing every quality and capacity of the grown man: his sex and size, his eye and hair color, his talent and intellect. Even his character will be molded by natural tendencies, and the map of his future is to a large measure already charted.

But for a moment, this first stage of life is purely physical. In the darkness of the womb, this first vestige of life is entirely devoted to the business of growing, to preparing for the life to come. There are eyes, but they do not see. There are ears, but they do not hear. Nerves do not feel; the brain does not think. The unborn fetus has many limbs and organs that are of no use to it now. Attributes and qualities lie dormant in the tiny being, never expressed, never revealed. Nonetheless, they exist, and they hint at the new kind of life to follow.

Finally, the time comes when the child must leave the shelter of the womb. He must undergo a transition, one that is every bit as traumatic as death itself. The child dies to this first stage of life in order to be born into a second stage. We might think that this would be a painful ordeal, but a kindly nature, a benevolent Providence, has arranged things for the best: the child feels no pain!

Now born, the baby opens his eyes and begins to realize that he has entered a second form of life, a new kind of life outside the womb. Suddenly, light attracts the baby's attention. His eyes follow it, blinking. He is fascinated. Noises startle him; he sniffs the air. He is overwhelmed by sensation; he begins to feel everything. He has entered the world of experience.

Soon the child can move about. He begins to discover the world of his second life. He can enjoy it, wonder at it, and gradually, understand it. This second stage of life is still very much like the first. It is still physical, but it offers the child a new opportunity: he can think! And slowly, the child realizes that he exists.

For many years, the child will develop his mind, reflecting, planning, learning, and reasoning. Each bit of knowledge is used to build more knowledge. He considers and concludes. He acquires wisdom.

But what then? The experience ends suddenly, like a light switched off. What happens to the man? Does he just die? Does he just stop?

There is an amazing parallel between the first and second stages of life, between the world of the womb and the world of experience. In the first stage, in the darkness of the womb, the child develops capacities and qualities that are of no use to him in his quiet, inky-black world. Exactly the same thing occurs during the second phase of life, this life. He also develops capacities that are superfluous to his present existence. As long as man lives, he requires no more than other animals. And yet, man searches, gropes, questions, and dreams beyond his reach. His nature inclines him towards good in this world, to seek a moral and ethical life, to try to serve G-d. Of what value are these qualities, these potential virtues? Are they simply for the grave?

Judaism says no! This life is not the end. We still have not experienced our final birth. We still live in a womb, a womb as dark and silent as the one surrounding the unborn child. We still live in a womb, but it bears another name; we call this womb a body.

In the womb, a mere cell develops into a human being. In the womb that is the body, a person also grows and develops. But this process takes longer — not the short nine months required by the fetus, but seven, eight, or nine decades: a lifetime! Physical growth is completed in a fraction of that period, but the full span is needed for the essential development of a human being: for 70, 80, or 90 years, we develop in spirit.

Every good deed, every kind word, every whispered prayer, every heartfelt insight nourishes this growth and adds to this development. Finally, when we are old and gray, the period of development ends, and the time comes for us to leave this womb, which we call our body. But now, finally, we are prepared for a new birth, a new existence. Finally, we are ready to stand before G-d.

Now imagine that an unborn child could think. Imagine that the child knew he must leave the womb, surrendering his warm secure life forever, never to return. The womb has been an integral part of his being, as our bodies are for us. He cannot conceive of life without it and so, giving up the womb seems to him to be giving up life itself. Imagine such an unborn child thinking about leaving the womb, worrying about it. For this unborn fetus, the idea of leaving the womb is just as frightening, just as terrifying, as death itself.

But we are wiser. We know that this unborn child is not really dying. We know that he is at last fulfilling the promise of his first life; that he is being born into a more significant life, into a world of brightness and light, into a world of experience.

The same is true when a person leaves the womb that is the body, when he dies to his present stage of life. He is born again into a third form of life, a life that pales this one in significance. Why should we fear death? Why should we doubt that a loving G-d, Designer of what we call nature, will make this second birth as easy and painless as the first?

I once heard a story about a little boy, an only son, who was stricken with an incurable disease. Month after month, his mother nursed him, read to him, played with him. She tried to keep him from realizing that his days were numbered. But as the weeks passed by, the little fellow grew worse and worse. He looked out of his bedroom window and saw the other children running and playing. He realized that he would never again be like them. He began to understand what his mother had tried so hard to hide. He knew that he was going to die.

One day his mother was reading to him about King Arthur and the Knights of the Round Table. She read about the king's glorious wars, of the many brave knights who met their death in noble battle. Then she looked up into the eyes of her little boy and she saw a question on his face. Silently, she closed the book. The little boy looked at his mother, and he asked the one question that she dreaded, the question that burned in his childish heart: "Mommy, what is it like to die? Does it hurt?"

The mother turned her head away, her eyes blinded by tears. She couldn't answer. She couldn't even think. She ran into the kitchen as if supper were about to burn. She knew that this question was vital, that her answer would have to comfort her only son through the last weeks of his life, and even beyond life.

The mother leaned against the kitchen cupboard, her knuckles pressed white against the woodwork. In unspoken prayer she asked G-d for the strength to tell her dying son the truth, the wisdom to know what to say.

Suddenly, it seemed as if she knew just what to answer her little boy. She returned to him and stroked his hair.

"Michael," she began, "do you remember when you were just a tiny boy, how you used to play so hard all day? When night came, you were so tired, too tired even to undress. You would tumble into Mommy's bed and fall asleep.

"But that was not your bed — it was not where you belonged — and you would only stay there for a little while. In the morning, much to your surprise, you would wake up and find yourself in your own bed, in your own room.

"Someone — someone who loved you — had taken care of you, and that's why you were there. Your father had come with his big strong arms and carried you away." The mother paused. "Michael, death is just like that. We wake up some morning and find ourselves in another room, our own room, where we belong. Our heavenly Father carries us there because He loves us."

The young boy smiled at his mother, his eyes shining. There would be no more fear, no more worry, only love and trust in his little heart, as he waited to meet his Father in heaven. He never asked again. And several weeks later, the little boy fell asleep, just as she had said.

The mother in this story searched for a parable which her small child could understand. But her simple answer reflects the deepest understanding of Judaism's wisest thinkers. In the Talmud, Rabbi Yaakov expresses this fundamental principle:

> This world is like an antechamber before the World to Come. Prepare yourself in the antechamber so that you may enter the banquet hall. (Avos 4:21)

So we pass through the antechamber, through the entry hall. The curtain is drawn open, and we live again.

When a baby is born, he escapes the confines of the womb, freeing his body to move and feel. So in this life, this third stage of existence, we are freed from the burden of our second womb, the body. Not with a wrinkled brow or a dimmed eye; not with a twisted spine or a withered arm; not with a mind haunted by endless fears, nor tortured with regrets; not with a heart torn by bitter memories, nor cut by the broken glass of shattered dreams: Not with these do we cross the threshold, not with these are we born into this new life.

We rise, never again to be encased in the dying clay of mortal flesh, but bright and clear, shining with the mercy of G-d.

With trust in G-d, we are not afraid, for there is nothing to fear. And when a person is no longer afraid to die, then he is no longer afraid of anything else. Only then, when we are no longer afraid, do we really begin to live. Then do we truly experience every joy and every pain. We begin to live and we are grateful for every moment of this life.

A man who is afraid of death is, to some extent, also afraid of life. But when death loses its fear, when it becomes worthwhile, then life becomes worth living as well. And when you have something worth living for — an ideal, a goal, a faith — then when death comes, it will come as a welcome friend, sent to usher us into a new life, a new birth.

> Even though I walk in the valley of the shadow of death, I will fear no evil, for You are with me. . . . May only goodness and mercy pursue me all the days of my life. (Psalms 23:4,6)

WHY AM I LIVING?

"Why was I born,
Why am I living;
What do I get,
What am I giving...?"

These questions are often asked by young men and women as they struggle to find a philosophy of life to follow. Adults occupied in pursuing a career or raising a family usually do not have time to think about these questions unless tragedy strikes. For most people, the onset of old age is when philosophical questions become uppermost in the mind.

Twenty-four hundred years ago, however, there lived a man who constantly sought answers to these questions. He was Socrates, the great Greek philosopher of Athens. As a young man, Socrates realized that almost all the people around him spent their lives in pretty much the same way. They sought fame, riches and pleasure, yet never once asked themselves whether those things were really important. Socrates found this attitude worrisome, for unless the question was raised and given serious thought, people would never really know whether or not they were doing the right thing. Their entire lives might be wasted pursuing useless or even dangerous goals.

Socrates felt that it was his duty to try to lead men to a nobler, more meaningful life. His goal was to cause the people of Athens to question their every action. He accomplished this by questioning friends and acquaintances, and drawing them into arguments, thus teaching them to consider what life was about. For his efforts he was charged with corrupting the youth of Athens.

In the year 399 B.C.E., Socrates was brought to trial, a description of which is given in *The Apology*, a work by Plato, a student of Socrates. Socrates stood before a court composed of five hundred and one citizens of Athens. The court had neither judge nor jury; trial was by a majority vote. After Socrates offered his defense, he was condemned to death by a vote of 281 to 220. Socrates' response to his sentence is one of the most noble speeches of all time. He said:

"I cannot keep quiet, for that is to disobey G-d. The greatest good for a man every day is to discuss virtue and other things of life. Life without inquiry has no meaning. The unexamined life is not worth living."

Socrates' philosophy is ironically illustrated in the following story. A Georgia bootlegger suddenly found that he had run out of liquor. His irate customers were calling and he was getting quite frantic since he stood to lose quite a bit of business. He searched his house and found some antifreeze and some other dubious "ingredients" and concocted them into a brew. As you might imagine, the results were disastrous: thirty people died.

The police captured the bootlegger and he was charged with thirty counts of manslaughter. When questioned by reporters, his only comment was, "Well, it sure makes a man think."

It is indeed possible that the bootlegger had never thought about life until he was trapped by it. Most of us never bother to think about the meaning of existence until we are struck by a deep personal tragedy. But G-d has given man an intellect, and to neglect to use it is a sacrilege against Him. Indeed, faith by itself, without thought or wisdom, is apt to be a very shallow faith. In the words of Rabbi Elazar ben Azaria, "Where there is no wisdom, there can be no faith. Where there is no faith, there can be no wisdom" (Avos 3:21).

When a person looks at the universe through the eyes of faith, he looks at the world with wisdom, and all things take on an added dimension. Just as a beautiful, symmetric crystal growing in a chemical solution bespeaks a law of nature, a law of chemical bonding, so does the existence of life tell us of a law of nature that makes the existence of man inevitable. Such a law implies that matter was created so that life, and eventually mankind, would be certain to be created. The very nature of matter tells us that the universe has a purpose, and that it is the work of a purposeful Creator.

When a man believes that there is a Creator, and that there is a purpose to this world, his endeavors to fulfill this purpose makes his life worth living. The existence of man, a creature who can look for purpose in life, is not a mere accident, but the most significant phenomenon in all creation. With that in mind, the concept of good and evil takes on awesome proportions. That which is in accordance with the purpose of creation is good; that which goes against it is evil. We are nothing less than partners with G-d in fulfilling His creation.

The world viewed, however, through the eyes of the man without faith has no purposeful Creator. In such a world, mankind is nothing more than an accident, with no more consequence than a bacterium or a stone. Man can be looked at as a vile infection on the surface of this planet. If there is no purpose to existence, then all our aspirations are nothing more than the mechanizations of molecules and cells of our brain. We would have no alternative other than to agree with the famous columnist, the late H. L. Mencken, who said, "Man is a sick fly, taking a dizzy ride on a gigantic flywheel."

Furthermore, in a world where there is no purpose, there can be no good or evil, for both of these concepts imply purpose. Without faith, all values become completely subject to the whim of the individual. Morality becomes merely a matter of convenience to be discarded when it does not serve one's immediate goal. If existence has no meaning, our attitude toward the world, our fellow man, and society in general, need be little more than, "So what?"

When a colleague suggested to Albert Einstein that the laws of nature might be a mere manifestation of chance, this great physicist replied, "I do not believe that G-d plays dice with the cosmos." To the wise man, it is only too apparent that there is purpose in nature. But where there is no faith, there is no wisdom. The old-fashioned materialist who is convinced that human life is without a goal, and that man is an irresponsible particle of matter engulfed in a maelstrom of meaningless forces, is a man who has no wisdom.

The brilliant philosopher, Alfred North Whitehead, best summed up the folly of such persons when he remarked, "Scientists who spend their life with the purpose of proving that it is purposeless, constitute an interesting subject of study." The heavens may declare the glory of G-d, but the fool sees only darkness.

We must realize, now, before the inevitable is thrust upon us, that life is supposed to be understood and appreciated; and that we should take an active part in fulfilling the purpose of creation.

MEET YOUR CREATOR

And the L-rd spoke to Moses, saying, "Speak to all the congregation of the children of Israel and say to them, 'You must be holy, for I the L-rd your G-d, am holy.'" (Leviticus 19:1-2)

To understand this quotation from the Torah, we must focus on the word, "holy." Precisely what does it mean? And furthermore, what does the Torah intend when it describes G-d as "holy"?

Ordinarily, when we think of something holy, we think of something that is dedicated to G-d. Thus, we would consider a holy person to be one who dedicates his life to serving G-d. Similarly, we call a Torah scroll holy, since its use is dedicated to the worship of G-d. However, if to be holy is to be dedicated to G-d, then describing G-d Himself as holy would seem to be meaningless, a senseless redundancy.

Delving deeper into the semantics of the word "holy" reveals another meaning. "Holy" actually means separated from earthly, worldly things. Thus, a holy person is not only dedicated to G-d, he also relinquishes all worldly things. A holy vessel is not simply used in a worship service; it is never used for any mundane purpose at all.

This, then, is what the Torah means when it describes G-d as holy. He is completely separated from all earthly things, from the physical and material world. His nature is beyond all human comprehension. Even the highest angels cannot fully understand G-d's true nature. Only G-d Himself can truly know Himself.

Maimonides describes this in his *Canon of the Laws of the Foundations of Faith:*

> Even the very highest spiritual beings cannot understand the true nature of their Creator.... Although their knowledge of G-d far transcends that of any mortal man — that of any creature bound to the physical world — still, there is no being, other than G-d Himself, who can understand the nature of G-d.
> (Ch. 1, Par. 8)

Such an analysis may indeed seem discouraging. Since by definition no one can ever hope to understand fully what G-d is, many people give up trying to understand Him at all. Yet, this attitude is not merely negative, it is in fact very wrong. Although we can never comprehend G-d's true essence, there are many things about Him that we do know.

What is G-d? To Whom do we address our prayers? Whom do we serve? These are questions about which we can learn a great deal.

Our first concept of G-d is that He is the Creator of the universe. "In the beginning G-d created the heaven and the earth" (Genesis 1:1). What does it mean to be the Creator of the universe? And what is this universe that G-d created?

The earth is a ball suspended in space. Its diameter is about 8,000 miles. If a man were to take a trip around the world, he would travel about 24,000 miles. Imagine trying to walk from New York to Chicago. Even after such a long walk, one would have travelled across a very small portion of the earth — about 1/60 of the distance around the globe.

Compared to man, the earth is very big. Yet, vast though the earth may seem to us, it is a mere speck in the greater vastness of space. Ninety million miles from the earth is the sun, a fiery ball of gas, 866,000 miles in diameter, and over a hundred times larger than the earth. Even the sun is a mere speck in the great expanse of space. There are billions and billions of suns, for every star in the sky is actually a sun, thousands of times bigger than the earth, yet so far away that it appears to be a mere point of light.

These figures baffle the mind — we simply cannot grasp the concept of millions of miles. An imaginary model will help us to comprehend it. Picture a huge giant, suspended in outer space. Between his fingers he holds a little ball — one inch in diameter — about as big as a ping-pong ball. That is the earth. On its surface are cities and people, but they could only be seen with a microscope.

About three feet from this little ball is another, the size of a pea. That would be the moon. The sun, on the other hand, would be nowhere in sight. It would be placed about a quarter of a mile away — a glowing ball, nine feet in diameter, about the size of a small car.

Nine planets, the solar system, rotate around the sun. The furthest planet, Pluto, would be about 13 miles away. Even a giant holding the earth between his fingers would have a long walk if he wished to visit all the planets in the solar system.

But what if the giant wanted to visit the nearest fixed star, Alpha Centuri — how far would he need to travel? Even a giant could never make the trip on his own. Even he would be forced to take a rocket ship, for in this model, with the earth scaled to a one inch ball, the nearest fixed star would still be 40,000 miles away! And many stars would be farther still, millions of miles away, even on such a reduced scale.

Comparing the earth to a ping-pong ball may help us conceive of the solar system, but beyond that, the model fails us. The distances still boggle the imagination, so a new measure is required. The one most scientists use in discussing interstellar space is the speed of light.

Light travels 186,000 miles per second — over 600 million miles per hour — a hundred thousand times faster than the fastest rocket. Light travels around the earth in 1/7 of a second, from the earth to the moon in 1 1/2 seconds, and from the earth to the sun in about eight minutes. Yet it would take light, even at this speed, over four years to reach the nearest fixed star. And to reach many of the stars we see in the sky, light would have to travel for many hundreds of years.

Each one of these distant stars is like the sun, thousands and even millions of times bigger than the earth. The stars cluster together in galaxies. In our galaxy alone, astronomers count over one hundred billion stars, each one thousands of times larger than our planet, many with solar systems of their own. Can we imagine the size of a single galaxy? It would take light, travelling at over 600 million miles per hour, over one hundred thousand years to cross our galaxy alone.

Yet this enormous galaxy, with its billions of stars, is but a speck in the universe. Modern telescopes can photograph hundreds of billions of galaxies, each one containing hundreds of billions of stars. Can the human mind begin to comprehend the size of even the visible universe?

Still, our universe is finite. Scientists proved that many years ago. Finite though it may be, the universe is so immense that it staggers the human imagination. Our planet, our solar system, even our galaxy, are like minute bits of dust in the vast expanse of the universe.

Where, then, did this vast universe come from? How did this tremendous amount of matter and energy come into being? There can be only one answer: It was created by G-d. Stars, planets, galaxies, billions and billions of them all — all were created by G-d! What great power G-d must have!

One might think that creating such a huge universe was a lot of work for G-d, even that it tired Him out. Nothing could be further from the truth. The Midrash tells us that G-d created the universe with the Hebrew letter *heh*. That is, G-d created the universe with as little effort as it takes to pronounce the sound "huh." G-d's power is infinite, so that for Him any finite task, no matter how enormous, is nothing.

Many people have asked, if G-d is so great, and if the entire universe is His domain, how can He pay any attention to the tiny speck of cosmic dust that is our planet earth. How can He give any consideration to the prayers, or to the actions, of any single individual? Such questions underestimate G-d, for just as He has infinite power, He also has infinite wisdom. Imagine: infinite wisdom, infinite intelligence, infinite mentality.

An ordinary human being has limited mental capacities. He can usually concentrate on only one thing at a time. Even then, his concentration may often waver and drift. Gifted individuals can occasionally concentrate on two or three problems at a time, but again, their concentration drifts from one thing to another; it is not absolute.

Suppose that the mentality of this entire planet were gathered, and the intelligence of all five billion people on earth were placed into a single mind. Presumably, such a mind would be able to concentrate on five billion things at once. Nevertheless, it would still be a finite intellect. But the intellect of G-d is infinite. G-d can concentrate His attention infinitely. He can focus simultaneously on every single atom in the universe. He is aware of each electron and each proton in all of creation, with less mental effort than a man uses to scan the newspaper.

An infinitely powerful G-d Who watches our every move, 24 hours a day — the implications are frightening. At every moment, G-d knows our every thought, for He sees not with light and eyes, as men do. Rather, He has an awareness of everything in the universe — an awareness that is much more than seeing — an awareness that only the Creator can have. It is a terrifying thought, but it is true.

When we first consider G-d's greatness, we are filled with tremendous awe. But if a person were to think a while, to realize just how great G-d really is, and if he would truly grasp how He watches us every second of the day, that person would become a saint. He would have no alternative. After all, how could a person do wrong if he realized that the Creator of the entire universe is watching him constantly and is interested in everything he does?

So it is indeed possible to know something about G-d. We know that He has infinite power and that He created the universe without effort. We know that He has infinite mentality, that He is interested in us, that He listens to our prayers, and that He loves His creatures. And we understand that there is only one G-d, for there can be only one Infinite Being.

We know that G-d has no body, no shape, and no form. Our very concepts of space and time become meaningless when we try to apply them to G-d's being. But G-d is not an abstract concept. He is very real, as real as we are. In fact, He is more real than we are, for our very concept of reality was created by G-d.

This, then, is the G-d to whom we all pray. When we pray, we are talking to G-d. We speak to the Being Whose power brought the entire universe into existence. We utter this thought in our morning prayers when we say, "Blessed is He who spoke and the universe came into being."

There is a story about the great Chassidic rabbi, Reb Zusia of Anipoli. He would always be the first to arrive in the synagogue each morning. One day, Reb Zusia was late. His students waited and waited. Finally, just before noon, he arrived, a look of awe and wonder on his face. The prayers began. Somehow they seemed more meaningful, more fervent than usual.

After the service, the students asked the rabbi where he had been. "We were so worried," they said.

Reb Zusia replied, "I will tell you. As you all know, every morning when we first awake we say the prayer, 'I give thanks before You, O Living and Eternal King, Who has returned my soul to consciousness in mercy. Great is Your trust.'

"This morning I began the prayer, 'I give thanks before You.' The thought struck me, what am I, and what is 'You'? Who am I to speak to G-d? How can I address the Creator of the universe?

"I began again. 'I give thanks before You' — I, an infinitesimal speck of creation, before You, the Author of all creation. I couldn't continue. It took me hours to gather courage to finish the prayer. That is why I was late."

Reb Zusia was overwhelmed by the implications of the brief and simple *Modeh Ani* prayer. Yet everytime we say a prayer, we are speaking to G-d Himself. We are standing before the Master of all creation, before the One Who created the earth, the sun, the stars, the entire universe.

In preparing to pray, we focus our minds on G-d's wonders, until we begin to realize to Whom we are praying. And like the Psalmist we exclaim,

> O L-rd, our G-d, how mighty is Your Name in all the earth...
> When I look at Your heavens, the work of Your fingers;
> The moon and the stars that You have established.
>
> (Psalms 8:2-4)

Through this awareness, we may fasten our gaze on G-d Himself, and with true feeling praise the Master of the universe:

> I will give thanks to the L-rd with my whole heart;
> I will tell of Your wonderful deeds...
> I will sing praise to Your name, O Most High.
>
> (Psalms 9:2-3)

PRAYER

To pray, do we have to be in a synagogue? Of course not! However, the synagogue can teach us how to pray. It can keep our spiritual mechanism well-oiled, so that it will not be rusty when we need it. Most people go to the synagogue to pray. There, we read from our prayerbooks, too often with little or no enthusiasm.

You can almost hear the dead, dry monotone of the responsive readings, for we do not know what prayer is, nor do we realize the great power there is in prayer. Here is a power so tremendous that with it, nothing is impossible; without it, nothing we do has any eternal significance. It is a power so simple that a child can use it. It is a power we can use with less effort than a thought. Despite its simplicity, the prayer of faith can move mountains, heal the sick, overcome the world — even work miracles!

Prayer is largely an unexplored field. The entire idea of communicating with the Infinite Power, G-d, has been little researched. The spiritual laws of prayer have not yet been discovered by the average person. Many regard prayer merely as an emergency measure or as a last resort when all else fails. Others regard prayer as a weekly ritual, a service attended very much like a subscription to a series of lectures. It is culture, not conviction, that keeps some people in the synagogue.

There is a deep fascination in exploring any new field. Every scientist feels it, and the explorer of spiritual realms will find it equally true. The great Chassidic rebbe, Rabbi Nachman of Breslov, devoted his prodigious energies to the art of prayer.

In his youth, he researched every known avenue of addressing G-d, from the common prayerbook to the most esoteric tomes. In his late twenties, he made a pilgrimage to the Holy Land, a perilous journey in those days. On the return trip, the Rebbe found himself stranded aboard a Turkish warship. During a fierce storm, while the crew worked vainly to pump the waterlogged vessel, the Rebbe's attendant approached him.

"Why don't you pray for us?" he cried, "I cannot even recite the prayers that I say every day, and certainly cannot open my mouth to G-d at a time like this. But you, Rebbe, know how to pray at all times."

The Rebbe replied, "I am now in a state of constricted mentality. I am far from G-d. But still, my council is faithful. We are now in fierce danger, and I have no other choice. G-d knows that I have never made use of the merit of my fathers, but now I am compelled." So, invoking the memory of his righteous grandparents, the Rebbe offered a brief prayer for G-d's help. For a moment, the danger seemed to increase as the ship headed into the tumultuous waves of a waterspout. Suddenly, a strong wind sped the ship forward and the clouds divided, allowing it to pass through safely. In gratitude, the Rebbe joyously recited psalms of thanksgiving.

The Rebbe's expertise in the ways of prayer enabled him to pray even when the situation made deep meditation and concentration impossible. But on that same voyage, Rabbi Nachman experienced an even deeper level of communication with G-d. Alone on a warship of Turkish troops, the Rebbe and his attendant were in grave danger of being robbed, imprisoned, and even sold into slavery. The thought was terrifying: What would he do if he were sold to a faraway place, a place with no Jews to redeem him? What if no one ever heard about it? Life would become unbearably difficult; it would become impossible to observe the Torah. As the Rebbe worried and pondered his situation, he began to accept it. Perhaps it was indeed possible to serve G-d, even as a slave in a foreign land.

If this was G-d's will, then he would continue to serve Him faithfully, despite the hardship.

As soon as the Rebbe had come to this conclusion, the sailors sighted land — the city from which the Rebbe was to be rescued. And while the Rebbe had hoped for nothing more than safety from the Turks, having accepted his peril as G-d's will, he soon found himself celebrating Passover as the honored guest of a great rabbi in a large Jewish community.

From Rabbi Nachman's experience, we see the workings of a rarely-understood spiritual law which always holds true. The prophet Jeremiah alluded to this law when he wrote, "Happy is the man who trusts in the L-rd, and the L-rd will be his trust" (Jeremiah 17:7). The Psalmist is even more explicit: "Cast your burden upon the L-rd and He will sustain you" (Psalms 55:23).

We must be willing to trust in the L-rd and seek to accept the will of G-d, no matter what it may be. Our prayers must not consist of efforts to bend G-d to our wills, but to yield ourselves to His, regardless of the consequences. A story is told about a Jewish businessman who lived in Poland. Business had been quite bad that year and he went to Rabbi Elimelech of Lezensk for advice. He complained to the rabbi that he had prayed and prayed for success, but success had never come. He asked the rabbi, "Why doesn't G-d ever answer my prayers?" Rabbi Elimelech answered, "G-d has answered your prayer. The answer was 'No.'"

We forget that sometimes even G-d has to say no. We pray to G-d as our heavenly Father who, like a wise human father, must often say "No." G-d does not deny us our wishes out of malice or caprice, but out of love and wisdom. He has full knowledge of what the future holds and what is in our best interest.

Many of our ancient prayers begin with the words, "May it be Your will, O G-d...." We must pray with the stipulation that G-d's will, not ours, be done. This is the factor of Divine decision that the skeptic cannot understand, but which the believer must accept. From this factor comes the prayer that is answered with "Yes."

Rabbi Menachem Mendel Schneerson, the Lubavitcher Rebbe, is considered one of the great Chassidic leaders of our time. Several years ago, a woman came to him for help. Her only son was desperately ill with leukemia, and it would be only a matter of months before he would succumb. The mother, trembling with fear, spoke to the Rebbe while tears rolled down her cheeks. The Rebbe looked into the mother's eyes and said, "If you knew that it was G-d's will, would you be willing to let your son die? Could you give him up if you knew that G-d wanted him?"

The poor mother just sat there, looking back at the Rebbe. After a long struggle with her emotions, she finally replied, "Yes, if I knew for certain that it was G-d's will, then I would be willing to give up the boy."

Rabbi Schneerson nodded and said, "Now we can pray for the boy." He then offered a prayer for the youth, surrendering him completely to the wisdom and mercy of G-d. Three days later the boy was released from the hospital. I knew the boy. He is a grown man now.

When we know how to pray, prayer has amazing power. When we learn to accept G-d's decisions, He is far more willing to give us the things we are anxious to have. The pitfall lies when, after praying and seeking an answer to our troubles, we refuse to pay attention to the answer that G-d gives us. We are like people who visit a doctor, only to ignore his advice unless it happens to coincide with what we wanted to do anyway. We can almost imagine G-d saying to us, "Behold, for many years now you have come to Me and asked to know My will. I have spoken, you have heard and you have promised. But then you have gone your way as if I had not spoken. Now you come again. Is this a game that you play with Me?" If our prayers are to be answered, we must be sure that they are not so weighted down with ego that they cannot possibly rise to heaven.

Some people seem to feel that if G-d does not grant their immediate wish, then He must not be a very good G-d. I am reminded of an anonymous quotation:

> I, I, I,
> Myself and I
> The inside and the outside,
> The what and the why;
> The when and the where,
> The low and the high;
> All I, I,
> I itself I.

There are many people who pray in the same fashion: Give me; grant me; do for me. The warp and woof of the entire fabric of their prayer seems to be I — me — my — mine, when in fact, prayer is exactly the time to forget about ourselves and our desires. It is a time when we should concentrate on Thee — Thou — Thy — Thine. If we were to place the emphasis where it belongs, then our prayers might be more promptly and favorably answered.

What enables us to stand before the Infinite G-d and ask Him to comply with our little wishes? Our sages taught us to begin our prayers by saying — and meaning — "May it be Your will, O G-d...." "If it is Your will to grant my prayer, so be it. And if the answer is, 'No,' You, O G-d, are wiser than I am." It may be just this vast difference between G-d and man thát makes many of us reluctant to pray. We may feel as Voltaire did, when he said, "G-d is like the president of a coach line crossing the continent in his private car. It is of no concern to him that ants are on the ground under the wheels of his coach." Voltaire, however, did not have the whole story. Though we may not understand it, man is unimportant, yet all-important. Man is nothing to G-d, yet everything.

This enigma is pondered in the Psalms:

> "When I behold Your heavens, the work of Your fingers,
> The moon and the stars which You have established,
> What is man that You remember him?
> Or the son of man that You think of him?
> And yet You have made him
> But a little lower than the angels.
> You have crowned him with glory and honor.
> You have set him above the works of Your hands."
>
> (Psalms 8:4-7)

This may be very difficult to understand, for in reality, we know very little about G-d. No matter how far we progress in our studies, we will never know G-d as He truly is. We do not know what G-d knows, or even how He knows. We only know enough about G-d to pray to Him and to trust in His wisdom.

When we pray we must realize to Whom we are praying, as it says in the Talmud, "When you stand in prayer, know before Whom you stand." When we say, "Blessed are You, O L-rd," we must know who "You" is, and we must realize what we mean when we say, "O L-rd." When we read the words of a prayer, we are not merely reading words in a book. We are speaking to Someone Who is listening to our words and to our heart.

In the Tractate of *Brachos* (13a), the Talmud tells us that we may pray in any language, since it is preferable to understand the words that we pray. Jewish prayer is not an exercise in uttering meaningless words; it is speaking with G-d from the very depths of the heart and being. Read slowly, understand what you say, contemplate the words, and realize to Whom you are saying them.

Prayer, whether it be in the synagogue, or in the innermost recesses of the heart, is not something to be taken lightly. When we pray we are speaking to G-d, and nothing is beyond His power. G-d has promised us, "Call upon Me, and I will answer you, and I will show you great and mighty things such as you have never seen before" (Jeremiah 33:3).

It is the chance of a lifetime!

HOW MAN CREATED G-D

Can you by searching find G-d?
Can you find out the Alm—ghty to perfection?

(Job 11:7)

The question put to Job seems very difficult. So let's begin with a simpler one: What is G-d? Perhaps this question also seems difficult, but really it is so simple that even a young child knows the answer. What is G-d? "G-d" is a word. A word with great meaning, perhaps, even of profound significance. But still, simply stated, "G-d" is a word.

On the other hand, a word is more than just a pattern of sounds, a random noise. Behind every word is a thing, an idea or a concept. So, when we say the word "G-d," we are speaking of something, of a reality. Just what is this reality? Just what do we mean when we say the word, "G-d"?

There are many words that are difficult to understand if we look deeply into their meanings. For example, let's examine the word "nothing." "Nothing" is also a word. But what is nothing? What does it look like? What do you see when you try to imagine nothing? Does it look black? But then, if it's black, it isn't nothing — it's blackness. A great thinker once said that nothing is what you see behind your head. So take a look. Without turning around, what do you see behind your head? Nothing.

Now that we know what nothing looks like, we can ask another question: Does nothing exist? Is there really such a thing as nothing? If not, if nothing is not a thing, then we can't really say that it exists, or at least not as we usually think of existence.

But does nothing exist? Common sense tells us that it does. After all, before there was anything, there was nothing. Before G-d created the universe, there was nothing — nothing, that is, except G-d.

It is very difficult to picture nothing. But G-d is even more difficult to imagine, even more impossible to picture. In the classic work of the Kabbalah, the *Tikuney Zohar*, the prophet Elijah is quoted as saying to G-d, "No thought can grasp You at all." The great Chassidic leader, Rabbi Shneur Zalman of Liadi, explains this idea. He writes that the human mind is not constructed or equipped to comprehend G-d. Just as you cannot hold a thought in your physical hand, so you cannot grasp G-d with your mind. Just as no hand, no matter how strong or large, can grasp any thought, no matter how simple, so no mind, no thought, can understand G-d.

So what do you do with a concept that you cannot grasp? What do you do with something so transcendental, so remote from our imagination, that the mind cannot even conceive it? First of all, you give it a name. You try to imagine how it affects you. You try to establish some relationship with it. This is what man did with G-d. And this is how man "created" G-d.

We cannot even begin to imagine G-d. But we do speak to G-d; we address G-d; we pray to G-d. We know that G-d has a relationship with the world, and that He continues to sustain and uphold it. So we invent a word and we call this word "G-d." We create an image, a concept, we say that this is G-d. But the real G-d, the real Creator, the Infinite Being, is so far beyond the grasp of our intellect that we cannot even begin to know it; we cannot even give it a name.

The Bible begins with the words, *"Berashis Bara Elokim Es HaShamayim V'es HaAretz"* — In the beginning G-d created the heavens and the earth." In the original Hebrew, the word "G-d" is the third word. It follows *"Berashis"* — in the beginning and *"Bara"* — created. The *Zohar* asks a very profound question about this first verse in the Torah. Why didn't it begin by saying, "G-d created heaven and earth in the beginning"? After all, G-d is the most important concept in the Torah. Why isn't He mentioned first?

The *Zohar* answers that until there was a beginning — a creation — the name of G-d could not be used. It could not be used because there was nothing to attach it to, nothing that the human mind could grasp. Creation is like a handle for men to hold: without it, there can be no conception of G-d, and there can be no name.

This concept is found in the familiar song, *Adon Olam*:

> *Adon Olam, Asher Malach Beterem Kol Yetzir Nivra*
> *L'es Nasah, Becheftzo Kol, Azay Melech Sh'mo Nikra*
> Master of the Universe, Who reigned
> Before anything was created;
> At the time that all was made through His will,
> Then He was given the name, King.

G-d was always King, even before anything was created. But what is a King without subjects? Can we grasp the concept or give it a name? Thus, before the universe was created, G-d was indeed King, but He could not be given the name "King" until Creation had taken place, until He had subjects.

G-d *did* exist before the universe, long before the first man began to use his mind. But man created the concept and invented a word, a name, in a feeble attempt to grasp the ungraspable, to comprehend the incomprehensible, to fathom the unfathomable.

Sometimes men create a false god, and because this god is false, men cannot believe in it, and they deny it. One may naively picture G-d as an old man in the sky, preferably with a long white beard, and then go on to reject that image. But before a man denies G-d, he must first know what sort of G-d it is that he doesn't believe in. What sort of G-d has he created that he can't believe in? Is it a Mary Poppins G-d, a fairy godmother who would magically make the world perfect overnight? A man would have every reason to deny such a god, when he sees all the evil in the world. Perhaps his god is a human rights worker, a flaming liberal or a staunch supporter of the establishment. Such a god, when he fails to produce on schedule, also deserves to be denied.

But if you try hard enough, if you search deeply enough, then you can begin to approach the truth. You can create a credible G-d, in whom you can believe. Plumb the depths of existence and ask the ultimate questions: Why does the universe exist? Why does man exist? Why is there meaning to life? If you find G-d in the answers to these questions, then you have discovered the G-d your forefathers "created," the G-d of Abraham, the G-d of Isaac, the G-d of Jacob.

But if you cannot find G-d in this way, if the G-d created by your ancestors has no meaning for you, then search still further. Probe and search the depths of your life, the source of your being, and your ultimate concerns, whatever you take seriously without reservation. In order to do this, you might have to forget everything traditional that you have heard about G-d, even the word itself. But if you know that G-d lies behind all being, behind all depth in life, behind all genuine concerns, then you know much about G-d. You have created a G-d that is meaningful to you, a G-d that can make your life more complete.

This is a G-d that you cannot deny. You cannot call yourself an agnostic or an atheist or an unbeliever. You cannot say that life has no depth, that life itself is shallow. You cannot think, "There is no meaning to my existence!"

If you could make these statements without hesitation, without qualification, then you would be an atheist. But otherwise, you are not. If life has any meaning to you, then you have already created G-d, a G-d that gives your life meaning. And the G-d that you have created is just another aspect of the true G-d, the infinite, the unknown, the unnameable.

In the beginning there was nothing — and there was G-d. But G-d could not be comprehended; He could not even be named. Then G-d created man and thought. G-d created meaning, depth and concern. And then man was able to create G-d.

That was in the beginning. But G-d continues to create the world, to uphold it. And man continues to create G-d. So now, search your soul. What G-d have you created?

WANTED: G-D DEAD OR ALIVE

Much has been said about the "G-d is dead" theology. To say that G-d is dead is by no means a trivial statement; it is most difficult to understand. What does it mean to say that "G-d is dead," or "G-d is alive"? Indeed, what do we mean when we say "G-d"?

Human language lacks the vocabulary with which to talk about G-d. Because of this void, we must use the only words we have, and therefore we speak about G-d as though He were a person. Even giving G-d a name is inaccurate. How can you name something that is not a "thing"? G-d is more real than existence, yet more elusive than nothingness. He is everywhere and nowhere. He is changeless, yet causes change. How can we identify something that exists outside of the realm of space and time, something that has absolutely nothing in common with anything else that exists?

We cannot say many things about G-d, but we can say many things *to* Him. Compare the idea of G-d to the concept of a direction. No one wonders what "up" looks like, or how high it is, or if there really is an "up." Similar questions become meaningless when we ask them about G-d. "Up" is a physical direction; G-d is a spiritual direction. It is the direction towards which all of man's most noble aspirations are turned. Our prayers are addressed in this direction, and our prayers are answered, not from a thing or a place, but from an infinite spiritual height.

Nevertheless, Scripture does describe G-d. The prophet Jeremiah wrote: "But the Lord G-d is Truth; He is the living G-d and the everlasting King. The earth trembles before His anger; the nations cannot stand His indignation" (10:10). What, or Who, is this living G-d?

A living thing can be biophysically defined as something that locally reduces entropy, that is, something that makes order out of disorder. In other words, a living thing is something that can take things from its surroundings which have no order at all, and make them part of a living thing, which is a high degree of order. In the Yom Kippur prayers, G-d is called *Chai Ha'Olamim*, the Life of the Worlds. G-d is the direction of the order that is responsible for natural law and the possibility of life.

Another characteristic of a living thing is unity: it is a unified whole, a whole that is more than the sum of its parts. We don't think of an animal as having four legs, a head, a body and a tail. We think of it as a unified being. The direction that we call G-d is a unified, organized whole. It is a living direction that moves men and brings together all of mankind's goals of love, truth and peace. G-d lifts up man by every aspect of his being. When a person worships such a living G-d, the supreme aim of his life becomes an unfolding towards G-d, and that means nothing less than becoming something that is completely human. This is what the Bible means when it says that man is created in the image of G-d. The direction that is G-d and the direction that is total humanity are one and the same thing. Man is not guided by just one or two ideals, but by an organic whole of many ideals that point in the direction that is G-d.

The Bible says that idols are dead gods, but not simply because they are made of stone and wood. Idol worshipers believe in a different god for each aspiration: a god of truth, a god of justice, of love, wisdom, beauty, peace and so on. Each god stands alone; there is no unifying factor, no organic whole. Therefore, they are dead. What about a G-d of religion? Religion is also only one among many of man's lofty ideals. G-d has, all too often, become a G-d of the synagogue, of prayer books and rituals. A G-d of religion is no different from any other god. A "house of worship" god is a dead god. If one no longer worships a Living G-d, it is because he no longer associates Him with all the fundamental problems of human existence. When he says that he believes in G-d, he merely takes it for granted that G-d exists, but he does not look to G-d to give his life meaning. When people say that they don't believe in G-d, they take it for granted that He does not exist. The believer and the nonbeliever have one thing in common: They both take G-d for granted. He does not cause them any sleepless nights. G-d does not cause them any serious concern because, for them, He is the dead god of religion.

It does not really make any difference whether or not one believes in such a god; it is impossible to distinguish between believers and nonbelievers unless they openly state their position. Even more tragically, belief in G-d does not make any difference with respect to religious observance. There are people who attend synagogue services who do not believe in G-d. They may believe in the "Big Man Upstairs" Who runs the show, but they feel that it could probably run just as well without Him. They are not really aware of G-d — they never seem to feel His presence. Because it is a dead god that they worship, they can do so in comfort, even though they have cast all true religious feeling aside.

Nevertheless, even a "house of worship" religion is better than no religion at all. Some glimmer of truth is still preserved, so that even a dead god can be brought back to life. We still need and want G-d, be He a living G-d, or a dead god of religion. G-d is still wanted, dead or alive.

KNOWING AND REMEMBERING

When I was a young man in my twenties, I had a strange feeling in my chest. It bothered me for a week or two, and then it started to worry me. Finally, I went to see a doctor, an internist I knew rather well. He gave me a complete physical examination and then called me into his office. His face was quite grim and his voice was solemn. It was then that he told me that I was going to die.

My face turned white and my heart began to pound hard. That old cliche entered my mind: "This is it!" All my thoughts fled before his awesome words: "Mr. Kaplan, you are going to die."

The doctor paused. Then, after a moment, he added, "Yes, you are going to die, fifty or sixty years from now. You're in perfect physical condition. A little Maalox for the stomach might help, though."

I went home, happy and relieved that the doctor had found nothing to be concerned about. But the incident gnawed at me. True, my doctor had a morbid sense of humor, and for a few seconds I had been terrified, more frightened than ever in my life. But why, afterwards, should I have been so upset? After all, I knew that I am mortal. It is a subject one doesn't like to think about but, rationally, I knew that like everyone else, my time would come. I hoped it would be a long way off, but it would come. Someday, I would die.

I began to analyze the doctor's diagnosis. On what was it based? The exam was a physical — he checked the workings of my body and found them in perfect condition, yet warned me that this state wouldn't last forever. But what was the real subject of his exam? From what perspective did he predict my fate?

When a biochemist looks at man, he sees a chemical composition, consisting of molecules and atoms which undergo complex interactions. These enable him to move, to grow, and to respond to his surroundings. But is this all that man is? A fire moves, consumes, and grows. It changes color and intensity as it interacts with its environment. Yet, in itself, a fire has no purpose. It has no will, no mind; you might say it has no soul.

From another angle, the biologist examines man and sees an animal. Like all other animals, he breathes, he eats, he excretes, and he reproduces. He consists of cells and organs, each one doing its part: a biological system. But what else could be included in this definition? A fly also breathes, eats, excretes, and reproduces. Yet, a fly has no purpose in life. It does not ask, "What am I?" It does not build great cities or conquer mighty empires. It neither hopes nor dreams. It lives for the moment: a crumb of bread, a bit of sugar, escape from the flyswatter. Is the life of a man of no more consequence than this?

Perhaps the argument is unfair. After all, neither the biochemist nor the biologist considers the special abilities of man's highly developed brain. So how does a neurologist view man? He studies the mind and finds a fantastically complex computer: an intricate maze of electrochemical circuits, conditioned by the environment and responding mechanically to external stimuli. But is this all that man is — a high-tech calculator? Can any person believe that his mind is completely governed by the laws of cause and effect? Is it possible that every motion, word, or thought is nothing more than the mechanical output of an electrochemical computer? Have we no more free will to determine our actions than a preprogrammed box of hardware?

Were any of these descriptions of man complete, then my doctor's words should not have frightened me. What fear, what sorrow is there in the extinction of a chemical reaction, in the completion of an animal's short life cycle, or in the shutdown of a computer? Why, if I were truly objective, would I care, even if the chemical, biological, or electrochemical loss were my own?

But instinctively, we know we are more than all this. And so we avoid the subject of death. We refer to it through euphemisms. We say that someone has "passed away" or "left us." And when we are finally forced to confront death, our own death, we are afraid, we are upset, we are even indignant. Our accustomed reliance on the cold objectivity of science fails us. Science cannot even pose the right questions; no wonder we are not comforted by its answers. So man turns to religion. Many a person who has never been in a synagogue calls the rabbi when he knows that he is going to die. A person who rarely prays will drop everything for a Yahrzeit service, to mourn his loved ones. Why is this so? Why does man turn to G-d when faced with death? Why does the soldier in a foxhole, surrounded by exploding shells, pray to G-d, although he has never prayed before?

No man has ever escaped death, but through G-d, and only through G-d, man can conquer death. Only G-d has promised that death is not the end of life. Only G-d has promised that death transforms life, that it is a reawakening, a beginning of a new life, an eternal life.

This view of death is inherent in the very way religion views man, a view much broader and deeper than those of the biochemist and the neurologist. The Bible explains the creation of man with an unusual metaphor: "G-d formed Man out of the dust of the ground and blew into his nostrils a breath of life; Man thus became a living creature" (Genesis 2:7). G-d has no body, shape or form. What is the purpose, then, of this anthropomorphic metaphor? Why does the Torah say that G-d blew a breath into man?

This passage is discussed in the commentaries of the *Zohar*.

When a person blows out, the breath comes from deep within him, from the innermost parts of his being. So, explains the *Zohar*, the soul of man comes from the innermost part of G-d, a spark of the Divine, a portion of G-d's own infinite Being.

The Bible certainly acknowledges the aspects of man which scientists have analyzed: "G-d formed man out of the dust of the ground" — out of the same elements contained in the earth: carbon, nitrogen, oxygen, and hydrogen. This is our biological system, our electrochemical computer. But then G-d endowed man with a spark of His own Being, with a G-d—like soul. Man, as religion views him, now has an affinity with the Divine.

This is the reason we sense that man, above all of creation, is not bound by the laws of nature, by the rules of cause and effect. "And G-d created man in His image," that is, in the spiritual image of G-d (Genesis 1:17). As G-d is not bound by natural law, so man transcends cause and effect. As G-d is free to act, so man alone is given freedom of will. And, as G-d is eternal, so man is granted the possibility of eternal life. Thus, religion provides a solution to the fear of death — all we need to do is believe.

☆ ☆ ☆

Now I understood how my doctor had been able to frighten me. The cold materialistic view of man, the narrow vision of the biochemist and the biologist, terrifies our deeper self-awareness. We live in a materialistic era which leaves little room for religious beliefs. The concrete measures of dollars and cents, of cost-effectiveness and efficiency, universally applied to all human endeavors, together with the amazing feats of scientific and technological progress, make it difficult if not impossible to imagine the abstract and the spiritual.

A regular member of my synagogue, an observant man, once asked me why I had abandoned a solid scientific career, a good salary, and a bright future, for the rabbinate. My answer astonished him. I said that G-d had a mission for me. He looked at me, his rabbi, incredulously. "Do you really believe in G-d?"

How is it possible for a scientist, a modern man, to believe in G-d? How can I take comfort in the promises of religion? Instinctively, like all men, the scientist recognizes man's free will, his special position above the natural order. But how does this fit with his objective, "scientific," view of things? Perhaps surprisingly, it fits very well. There is much in the discoveries of scientific research which redirects the scientist back to G-d. Even within the phenomena he observes and studies, the scientist finds evidence of G-d's presence.

One of the most basic laws of physics is the Second Law of Thermodynamics. In simple language, this law states that it is easier to destroy than to build, that chaos proceeds from order rather than the reverse. This is not a mere moralism or philosophical conjecture, but one of the most firmly-based laws of physics, one which defines the very ordering of time. Order flows into disorder; energy tends to seek its lowest level.

Yet, despite this immutable law, we find a wonderful degree of order in the universe. Stars, nebulae, galaxies — all exhibit an astonishing variety of structure. Living creatures are composed of increasingly complex systems, from the simple-celled bacteria to the fantastically structured systems found in mammals. And the most complex, most perfected system is the human being, who is able to control and dominate the simpler systems and creatures which surround him.

The Second Law of Thermodynamics states that matter seeks its simplest state, yet the world exhibits a vast structure of increasing complexity. Some scientists label this a manifestation of anti-chance. But it could only be an infinite Intelligence that could bring order out of a chaotic universe. And this infinite Intelligence is nothing other than G-d. Man ascends not by the blind groping of chance, but by the inevitable ordering of the universe imbued in creation by G-d.

Man, at the apex of complex life forms, is qualitatively different from all those below him. The distinction, however, is hard to articulate; apparent definitions which pinpoint one or another human characteristic are often not confirmed by research into the abilities of various animals. Traces of dexterity, speech, communication, and even emotion seem to exist in various creatures. But we recognize that there is a fundamental distinction, and the Bible clarifies it for us: G-d blew into man a soul of life.

What is this soul of life? How does it distinguish man from the rest of creation? We know that all matter has a degree of divine sustenance. This is implied in the second sentence of the Torah: "And the spirit of G-d hovered on the face of the water" (Genesis 1:2). Even the most inert matter contains an essence of G-d's sustaining spirit. This returns us to the First Law of Thermodynamics, which states that matter and energy are eternal, that they cannot be destroyed. It is G-d's essence that gives them this permanent existence.

G-d's presence is apparent in all of material creation; this is what sustains existence. But as we examine most complex forms of existence, we find greater manifestations of G-d's essence. And finally, in man, G-d's essence reaches its zenith of expression, for man is created in the spiritual image of G-d. It is this Divine essence in man that we call a soul. And just as the First Law of Thermodynamics tells us that matter and energy are indestructible, due to the sustaining spirit of G-d, so the personality, the soul of man, is eternal.

Man's conscious life does not end in death; it merely assumes a new form, unencumbered by material flesh. The body may die, but the spirit lives on. We can ask the physician, the biologist, and the neurologist, "What has happened to a person who has died? Why is he still? Why is he lifeless?" They will answer that the heart has stopped beating, the blood supply to the brain was cut off, and certain minute chemical changes have occurred in the brain. A living organism has been transformed into a piece of inert matter. What was once a thinking, aspiring human being is nothing more than a dead husk. But we have G-d's promise that this picture is incomplete, that the breath of life which created man will sustain him, body and soul, eternally. This promise was given to the prophet Isaiah: "The dead shall live, the deceased shall rise. Awake and sing you that dwell in the dust" (Isaiah 26:19). The promise was repeated to the prophet Daniel:

> And the many that sleep in the dust of the earth shall awake, some to everlasting life, and some to disgrace and everlasting shame. And the faithful shall shine brilliantly like the brilliance of the heavens, and they that bring many to righteousness shall be like the stars, forever and ever. (Daniel 12:2)

What, then, happens when a man dies? Our observation of death inclines us to the view of the physician, that a man becomes a mere lifeless corpse. It is indeed true that certain minute chemical changes occur in the tissue of the brain. When this happens, the soul loses all contact with the body — the receiving mechanism is dead. The soul, an entity consisting of pure spirit, pure thought, is now free. The Bible describes this phenomenon in the Book of Ecclesiastes: "The dust shall return to the earth as it was, and the spirit will return to G-d Who gave it" (12:7). The body deteriorates and returns to the elements of the earth.

What happens to the soul after death, after it is separated from the body? Again, science cannot help us here, for it cannot explain what it cannot observe. But G-d has revealed to His prophets that in the life after death, there is a judgment, that there is a reward for good and a punishment for evil. This was suggested in the prophecy of Daniel, that those who "sleep in the dust of the earth shall awake, some to everlasting life and some to disgrace and everlasting shame." For this reason, our sages warn us to overcome our inclination to forget our mortality, and insist that we remember the day of our death. But we are also instructed not to fear or despair. We believe that G-d is just, rewarding good and punishing evil. If a good man suffers in this world, he will be rewarded in the World to Come. If an evil man prospers in this life, his punishment is due in the afterlife. For twelve months, the soul is judged and punished for its sins. After that, the punishment is complete, and the soul is ready for its eternal reward. The only exception to this is in the case of an atheist, a scoffer, or a blasphemer, for whom the punishment is eternal, a "disgrace and everlasting shame."

What, finally, can we expect after the period of judgment? What is life like in the world of pure spirit? Here, even revelation provides no answers, for it is beyond our understanding. The greatest Jewish philosopher, Moses Maimonides, wrote:

> The reward in the afterlife is not within the grasp of the human mind to understand — only G-d knows its full greatness, beauty, and substance. While the prophets may have written about a future world, they were prophesying regarding the days of the Messiah. There is nothing in human understanding that can compare to the life after death — no prophet can picture it — no mortal words can describe it.
>
> (Laws of Repentance 8:7)

His words confirm the prophecy to Isaiah: "Never has such been heard, and not perceived — no eye has seen it other than G-d — all that He shall do for those who trust in Him" (Isaiah 64:3). No prophet has ever seen the afterlife, nor has any mortal being. It is the realm of G-d alone.

We do not know exactly what the afterlife is like. We will find out when we get there. We do know, however, that G-d has promised that it is a life of divine reward, of sublime ecstacy. G-d has promised that nothing in human experience, whether of the senses or of the mind, can compare with the joy, the happiness, and the delight that the soul of a man experiences when it is close to G-d in the spiritual world.

Realizing the reality of one's own death, whether now or in 60 years, may be fearful and terrifying. It may make us sad or depressed to imagine leaving all the things to which we have devoted our lives — our homes, our fortunes, and our loved ones. But there is an answer. All we have to do is believe. All we have to do is remember G-d, remember His promise, remember our souls.

PART TWO

THE JEW AND SOCIETY

WHY IS A JEW?

> For I am the L-rd your G-d, who stirs up the sea, and makes its waves roar — the L-rd of Hosts is my name. And I have put My words in your mouth, and I have covered you in the shadow of My hand, that I may plant the heavens, and lay the foundations of the earth, and say to Zion, "You are My people."
> (Isaiah 51:15-16)

Different peoples have different calendars which reflect the essence of their uniqueness. Each calendar's beginning is marked by the most special event in that people's history. According to the Moslem calendar, it is now the year 1410, counted from the Hegira, Mohammed's flight from Mecca. On the Christian calendar it is 1990, counted from the birth of Jesus. But the Jewish calendar starts with the creation of Adam and civilization 5750 years ago. It dates back before the advent of recorded history, with the possible exception of the Bible. There is no era in the story of mankind in which we do not find some evidence of our people.

The world's first great civilization, Mesopotamia, or Ur, produced the first Jew, Abraham, almost 4000 years ago. Our people witnessed the rise and fall of all the great nations of the pagan era: Babylonia, Persia, Phoenicia, the Hittites, the Philistines, Greece and Rome. Of all the great civilizations, none has endured except one. History has thrown many challenges at our people and each one has been a threat to our very survival, but each has been overcome and the Jewish people have endured, to face the next challenge.

The existence and survival of the Jewish people has been one of the world's great mysteries. Historians have written volumes about it; philosophers have sought reasons for it; social scientists have tried to justify it; but still, the mystery remains. Why have we born the brunt of every persecution that the world could inflict and why have we survived it all? Why have we had the longest and most turbulent history of any group of people on the face of this planet? What strength and goal has maintained our existence to this day, enabling us to ponder the question?

Even our beginnings are mysterious. Historians throw up their hands in anguish when they try to trace the beginnings of the Jewish people, because there was no real recorded history when we got started. The Bible gives us some hints, but supplies few details: A patriarch Abraham, a family of Jacob's twelve sons, then a tribe of seventy families, and almost overnight, a nation of over three million. We see events thrown before us like flashes of lightning — slavery in Egypt, a miraculous exodus, the revelation at Mount Sinai, forty years in the wilderness, the conquest of Canaan — and suddenly we see Israel as a mature nation with a secure government.

As we look back at our turbulent history, we ponder our destiny and we ask, Why? Why is a Jew? Why do the Jewish people still exist? Why this miracle? I once heard a very interesting story that may point the way to an answer. The emperor of Prussia, Frederick the Great, was a philosopher and writer. Once, during a learned discussion with his Lutheran pastor, they found themselves discussing the question of G-d's existence. Every "proof" argued by the pastor was quickly refuted by the nimble mind of King Frederick. The emperor was tiring of this endless discussion. He asked the pastor for just one visible sign that no one could possibly refute. The pastor closed his eyes and thought long and hard. King Frederick became impatient and asked again, "Is there anything at all that I can see with my own eyes that would prove the existence of G-d?" The pastor suddenly opened his eyes and answered with just two words: "The Jews!"

This story provides us with a very important concept. If the survival of the Jewish people is indeed a miracle, then there must be a worker of this miracle. The miracle of our existence points a finger directly at G-d. A similar concept is found in the *Midrash Tanchuma* where we find a dialogue between the Roman Emperor Hadrian and the great Jewish sage, Rabbi Joshua. The Midrash tells us that Hadrian once said to Rabbi Joshua, "Great indeed must be the lamb, Israel, that it can exist among seventy wolves." Rabbi Joshua replied, "Great is the Shepherd who rescues her and protects her" (*Toldos* 5).

If a person were to see a flock of sheep existing and surviving among all sorts of dangerous, wild animals, he would know that the shepherd could not be very far off. When we see the Jews existing, surviving and even flourishing in the face of every possible hardship, and in spite of the most vicious enemies possible, we also know that our Shepherd cannot be very far off. When we ask the question, "Why is a Jew?" and seek the solution to the mystery of our destiny, we find ourselves confronted with an awesome concept: We are nothing less than witnesses to G-d's very existence. We stand before the world as a measurable phenomenon and we bear witness that the Shepherd is indeed very close.

The great prophet Isaiah expressed this concept most concisely and beautifully when he proclaimed: You are My witnesses, says the Lord, and My servant whom I have chosen, that you may know and believe Me and understand that I am He. Before Me there was no G-d formed, and none shall be after Me. I, even I, am the Lord, and besides Me there is no savior (Isaiah 43:10-11).

Therefore, we bear a tremendous and frightening responsibility. If our very existence must bear witness to G-d, then we must be certain to be good witnesses. If we do not act as befitting our mission, not only do we give ourselves a bad name, we also give a bad name to our Protector.

The Talmud discusses the question of sin, classifying various categories according to the level of severity. It enumerates the different kinds of evil that a person can do, and at the end of the list is the sin of doing something that gives a bad name to the Jewish people or the Jewish religion. The Talmud speaks about a religious person who is not absolutely honest in all his business dealings, and about the religious leader who does not set a perfect example of piety: These are counted among the very worst sinners. Since our mission is to bear witness to G-d, anything that gives the Jewish people or religion a bad name perverts this mission. Such actions are called "Chillul HaShem" — the desecration of the Name of G-d. A person who does this is not merely doing something bad; he is perverting the very reason for our existence.

In discussing this concept, the Talmud quotes from Isaiah. The prophet lambasts his people for turning away from G-d: And in that day did the Lord, the G-d of Hosts, call... and beheld joy and gladness, slaying oxen and killing sheep, eating flesh and drinking wine, "Let us eat and drink, for tomorrow we shall die!" And the L-rd of Hosts revealed Himself in my ears: "Surely this sin will not be forgiven until you die" (Isaiah 22:12-19). Here, again, the words of the prophet are clear: Since we are truly G-d's witnesses, we must live for much more than material joy and gladness.

Why is a Jew? A Jew is to bear witness that a people that serves G-d, and sets a good example to the world, can survive no matter what the world may throw at it. One of our great mystical books, the *Tikuney Zohar*, teaches that the Jewish people are like the wick in a lamp, and G-d's teachings are like the oil (Tikun 21:60a) As long as the flame burns brightly within us, we will spread the light of G-d throughout all the world. This is our secret. This is our destiny.

THREE TRUTHS

The L-rd G-d, is Truth (Jeremiah 10:10).
The very seal of G-d is Truth (Talmud, Shabbos 55a).

Truth — thoughtful people search for it; sincere people hope to set their lives on a true course. This has been the goal and purpose of thinkers and philosophers throughout the ages. But for Jews, it is not merely a question of intellectual curiosity or lifestyle. It is central to our religion, a defining characteristic of G-d. In fact, we are actually commanded to seek the truth at all times, to flee from falsehood:

Keep away from anything false. (Exodus 23:7)

But what is truth? There are so many people with conflicting ideas of just what truth is. Whose ideas satisfy the criteria of this mitzva? What is the truth we must seek? And, in this world of illusion and distortion, is it possible to separate truth from fiction? Will we even recognize the truth when we do see it?

There are three basic types of truth. The first is the truth of the mind, the truth of the intellect. It is the result of pure reason, following the laws of logic. This is the truth that the scientist seeks in the laboratory, that the mathematician discovers in his calculations; it is the truth that the philosopher probes in the depths of his mind. Yet this truth is not abstract. It enables us to build bridges and skyscrapers, to design airplanes and rocket ships. This is the truth of logic and rationality, which distinguishes the civilized man from the superstitious savage.

But man does not live by logic alone. A life of pure reason

would be extremely dull, even meaningless. Man is a being of feeling and emotions; he lives through his senses. Therefore, we recognize a second type of truth: aesthetic truth.

When we say that a symphony is a great work of art, or that a painting is beautiful, we are telling the truth, although no scientist can prove it in his laboratory. Logic doesn't explain why the sight of a beautiful sunset lifts the soul; reason can't analyze our impulse to call a rose lovely. Nevertheless, beauty has a truth of its own, a truth sought after by artists and poets, a truth we all know, but cannot understand.

Yet even beauty cannot give meaning to life. What beauty is there in a life doomed to death and decay? And so, man searches for a third truth: Divine truth. This is the truth revealed to us by G-d. Our minds cannot discover it; our senses do not experience it. It is the truth found in the Bible, explained by the prophets. We recognize this truth when we have a feeling of closeness to G-d, whether in prayer or when observing His commandments. Just as man trains his mind to be logical, or opens his heart to beauty, so must he untether his soul to recognize Divine truth. It is Divine truth that tells us that we are human beings, and not merely animals that think or machines which feel. And it is Divine truth which has been sought after and recognized by all human cultures.

Analyzing the types of truth helps us to know what we are looking for. But how will we be certain when we have found the truth? How will we know it? Most people assume that their minds are logical, and that their logic is infallible. They think they will be able to recognize the truth when they see it. They believe that their minds function truthfully, like a computer, and that the data the computer processes, the evidence of the senses, is also true. After all, seeing is believing.

Or is it? Optical illusions are so commonplace that they no longer amaze us. But logical illusions are even more common. Fallacies, inconsistencies, double-talk — our minds are saturated by them all. The truth is that the average man is quite illogical.

How much are our thoughts really governed by reason, and to what extent are they influenced by the environment? A psychologist named Asch designed an experiment to determine the answer to this question.

Asch's experiment was conducted on a large college campus. Seven individuals were brought into a room and told that they were to be tested on their perception, on how well they were able to judge sizes. Of these seven people, only one was really being tested, but not for perception. The other six were assistants, paid by Dr. Asch to try to confuse the real subject of the test. But he, of course, didn't know that.

The seven people sat down in a room. On the wall was a chart on which two lines were drawn. One line was ten inches long, while the other was twelve inches. The lines were close to each other, and it was quite obvious that the twelve inch line was longer.

Each person was then asked which line was longer. The six assistants were asked first. Each one confidently stated that the ten inch line was the longer of the two. When the actual subject was finally asked his opinion, the study found that in 60% of all cases, he would agree that the ten inch line was longer than the twelve inch line.

What happened to a subject who didn't agree, who belonged to the independent 40% who still insisted that the twelve inch line was longer? The six hired assistants would laugh at him, ridiculing his obvious mistake. The more the subject would insist, the more the assistants would tear him down. The study found that under such pressure, another 30% would finally admit that the ten inch line was longer than the twelve inch line.

This study tested both college students and professors. It demonstrated conclusively that under enough social pressure, nine out of ten people could be convinced that a ten inch line was longer than a twelve inch line. In the end, they would even defend their conclusion vigorously.

When interviewed later, the subjejcts had all sorts of excuses: perhaps it was the angle from which they viewed the chart, or their eyes hurt that day. They were very uncomfortable when told that they had been duped, but duped they were. Think of it! Only one person out of ten was able to uphold his conviction that a twelve inch line is longer than a ten inch line.

We have the advantage of hindsight. We know both the design and the results of the study, and can confidently assume that we would never have been so duped! But is that so? Unfortunately, most of us do belong to the 90% who give in. Otherwise, it wouldn't be 90%. We tend to think as our neighbors think, to believe the things our friends believe. Very few of us have taken an unpopular stand among our friends, or have stood up for our convictions in the face of strong social pressure. Very few of us are able to oppose the crowd.

Our search for truth is often clouded, even blinded by group pressures. This is especially true of the search for Divine truth. Attendance at a house of worship may be fashionable nowadays, but deep religious convictions are not. A person with deep religious convictions must often withstand intense group pressure.

Only too often, we tend to reject the basic teachings of our religion, not because they lack logic, but because they lack popularity. If we want to hold true to our faith, we must think for ourselves. But how often do we succeed?

"If you repeat a lie often enough, people will believe it." Adolf Hitler (may his name be blotted out) proved the power of his favorite saying by transforming a nation of decent, logical, aesthetically sensitive people into a gigantic madhouse, one of the bloodiest nations in history.

Repeat a lie often enough, and people will believe it. Ninety percent of all people are influenced by group pressure. Only one out of ten will think for himself. Are you that one?

How will we know the truth when we see it? Logic fails us; aesthetics changes with the times. And our deepest convictions are drowned out by the roar of the crowd. So the search for truth, for all truths, but especially Divine truth, requires strength, requires every bit of stubborn resistance we have. But most of all, it requires aid, Divine aid. And so the search is begun with a plea for help: "Purify our hearts to serve You in truth" (Prayerbook). Only with such help can we hope to be successful.

LET NOT GUILT BE YOUR RUIN

I once heard a prominent psychiatrist discuss the psychological aspects of suicide. It is very difficult to understand suicide, for when you come down to it, it is very hard to imagine how a person could actually take his own life. To what depths of despair must a person be driven before he can destroy his very existence? What goes on inside the mind of a person when he decides to take this final, fatal step? The psychiatrist pointed out that many suicides stem from unresolved guilt resulting from a sin against his fellowman, or against G-d, or even against himself. His feeling of guilt is too great for him to bear and he starts to entertain thoughts of non-existence. The destruction of his very being becomes, in his mind, a pleasant alternative to a life burdened by this powerful feeling of shame. He knows of no other way to escape his guilt, no way to start anew, and so his only means is to end it all.

This point was once brought home to me with electric clarity. When we were living in Washington, there was a family in our building with whom we were friendly. We didn't know at the time that the husband was unfaithful to his wife. He kept his secret very well, but he couldn't conceal his shame from himself. Who can imagine the hell-fires that were raging in his mind? Torn between his guilt and his desires, the strain was too great for him. One night he took the family station wagon to a deserted area, ran a hose from the exhaust into one of the windows, carefully stuffing the space around it with blankets, and let the motor run. His body was found the next morning, his face flushed with the pinkish hue characteristic of carbon monoxide poisoning. He left behind a widow and four orphans, and we asked ourselves, which was worse, cheating on his wife or leaving a widow with four pathetic, fatherless children? How, we wondered, could this man take his own life when he had so much to live for?

For that matter, we wondered, how could anyone? Surely any kind of life would be preferable to committing suicide! But we do not understand the power of the human conscience, the inner self that judges our actions. At best it can be a severe judge; at worst, a merciless tyrant.

Every one of us has some moral code, some sense of right and wrong. We all feel that we have some sort of conscience, some guidepost on the path of life. It is interesting to note that even those who claim not to believe in G-d proclaim that they believe in the idea of right and wrong. Indeed, they often insist that they honor the dictates of their conscience more closely than do those people who believe in G-d. Certain agnostics go so far as to say that the reason they do not believe in G-d is not because they love religion less, but because they love conscience more! There are many people who claim that they do not believe in the human soul, but they hold on firmly to the idea of a human conscience, to their inner concept of good and evil. Can you imagine a greater paradox? The very people who reject G-d, who reject the soul, can still revere the conscience which is the voice of the soul, the inner voice of G-d.

Just what is this wonderful, mysterious tyrant, this inner despot, this human conscience, that raises its voice whenever we disobey it, and can drive man to despair and even death? A child once said that conscience was "what felt so bad when everything else felt so good." The many philosophers and moralists who have studied the human conscience have hardly arrived at a better definition. The German philosopher, Arthur Schopenhauer, tried to analyze it as one would analyze a chemical compound. He declared that the human conscience was composed of equal parts of fear, superstition, prejudice, vanity, and custom. Most of us, however, have loftier concepts of this inner voice. We hold it as the supreme judge of what is good and what is bad, what is right and what is wrong.

Even those timid agnostics, who half believe that they half believe, and who half doubt the substance of their own half doubt, have some belief in the conscience, even without G-d and without the soul. Of course, this is utter nonsense. If there is no G-d, then nothing is either good or bad; there is no right nor wrong. Any concept of a conscience that purports to tell right from wrong, good from bad, is nothing more than an illusion. If there is no soul, then man is nothing more than a brute animal, and, disguise the ugly fact as you may, a brute animal can have no conscience. If we get rid of G-d, if we cast away the human soul, if we still want to be logical, we must go all the way and get rid of all concepts of right and wrong, all ideas of conscience. We cannot eat our spiritual cake, and still try to hold onto it. But no matter what its origin, we all have some feeling within us that some things are right and others wrong; that some are good and others bad. We all feel the pangs of our conscience, that voice within us uttering judgement upon our deeds. It is a judge that condemns without mercy, banishes without appeal. It can often sentence us to a lifetime of imprisonment in a self-made cell of guilt and shame. For many people, the only exit from this prison is suicide, be it the suicide of taking one's life, the suicide of alcohol and narcotics, the suicide of a nervous breakdown, the suicide of withdrawal and mental illness, the suicide of dedicating one's life to escaping from life. When a person accepts his own conscience as his sole judge, the only escape from its jurisdiction is an escape from life itself.

The famous soliloquy of Hamlet expresses this entire concept in timeless poetry. Hamlet is torn by doubt, fear and guilt, and he cries out the question that is on so many tongues:

> To be, or not to be: that is the question.
> Whether 'tis nobler in the mind to suffer

> The slings and arrows of outrageous fortune,
> Or to take arms against a sea of troubles,
> And by opposing end them.
> To die, to sleep —
> No more — and by a sleep to say we end
> The heartache and the thousand natural shocks
> That flesh is heir to! 'Tis a consummation
> Devoutly to be wished. To die, to sleep....
>
> (Hamlet IIIi; 55-64)

Man is his own severest judge. Suppose we would want to completely satisfy our conscience, to make atonement for all the wrongs that we have ever done. Can you imagine what a task it would be? We would have to think back, to remember all the words we had ever said that had hurt someone, words that had given pain, that had cut like a whip into a sensitive heart, words that had given anguish to a friend, to one we love. We would have to walk up to each and every person whom we had hurt with words, to gather up their pain and lay it on our own hearts. We would have to remember all the things we had ever done; all the things of which we are now ashamed; all the deeds that wounded others, that took away some of their joy and peace, that brought them pain. We would have to say to our own conscience, "I am guilty of all these things. Let me bear the punishment that I justly deserve." The tribunal in our own heart would fix the penalty: how much suffering we should bear, how much punishment we should take, what punishment for breaking someone's heart, for telling a lie, for harboring an unworthy suspicion, for saying a cruel, unkind thing. How much would it be? If we were able to recall each year, each month, each day, of our life, and if our own conscience, fully wakened and without mercy, were to lay upon us the just punishment for all our wrongdoings, our heart would be crushed, for we would not be able to bear its weight. We would scream out with the agony of Cain, "My sin is too great for me to bear!" Perhaps the Psalmist felt these same pangs of remorse when he exclaimed, "For my life was spent in sorrow, and my years in pain, my strength failed, *because of my sin*, and my bones are consumed" (Psalms 31:11). However, the Psalmist continues, "But I trusted well in You, O L-rd, and I said, 'You are my G-d'" (31:15).

Many people feel that they can live out their lives without a formal religion by setting their own standards of morality. Of course, every man can design his own code of conduct and standard of ethics, but what happens when he fails to live up to his own high standards? His very flesh and bones can be consumed by his guilt. His sin can be his very ruin, for there is no one who can pardon him.

Our era, in which so many rely only on their own conscience, has become an era of tranquilizers and pep pills, of nervous breakdowns, alcoholism and drug addiction. Among the orthodox Jews of yesteryear, among people who lived by a code of conduct far stricter than our own, these upheavals were much less common. When a person accepts Divine law, a G-d—given code of morality, he is no longer forced to suffer the tyranny of his conscience. Only G-d, the Father of all mercies, the Compassionate Tribunal, is his judge. The same G-d who has taught us what is right and what is wrong, has also taught us that when a person regrets his sins and repents, he is forgiven. This is what G-d told King Solomon after the first Temple in Jerusalem was completed: "And if My people, over whom My Name is called, shall humble themselves and pray and seek My Face and turn from their wicked ways, then I will hear from heaven and I will forgive their sin " (Chronicles II 7:14).

Each person can choose how to live his life. He can be his own judge, subject to the rule of a cruel and pitiless conscience, scourging him with the fiery whips of guilt, or he can accept G-d as his judge, a merciful and compassionate G-d, slow to anger, and full of mercy. To be your own judge means to live without hope of pardon, while to accept G-d as your judge is to open the gates of pardon and forgiveness, to be able to start anew and to wipe the slate clean. G-d knows that mortal man can never completely live up to any code of law, be it self-imposed or Divine, and, therefore, unless there is a means of personal renewal, some way in which a person can cleanse himself of sin, he will never be rid of the awesome power of guilt. We find a Talmudic saying in the name of Rabbi Ishmael, "If not for the fact that G-d created repentance, if every day He did not stretch out His Hand to receive those who return to Him, then the world could not exist."

The faithful Jew is not bound by his sin. He can always turn to a willing and forgiving G-d Who can be approached at any time, be it alone in his room at night or in the midst of his fellow worshipers, to confess his sin before the Alm-ghty and ask forgiveness.

G-d has given us this promise through His prophet, Isaiah: "If your sins are red as scarlet, they can become white as snow; if they are red as crimson, they can turn as white as wool" (Isaiah 1:18). "If you seek the L-rd your G-d, you shall find Him when you seek Him with all your heart and with all your soul" (*ibid.* 43:25).

The nonbeliever does not have the freedom to choose this life-enriching liberation from guilt. He must seek the escape of nonreality, narcotics, or the oblivion of suicide. But a person should never think that just because he has kept himself away from G-d all his life that he has no hope. Nothing could be further from the truth! In his canon on repentance, Maimonides writes that even if a person were to spend a lifetime blaspheming and sinning against G-d, He is always willing to accept him back, to wipe the slate clean and to let him start anew. Whether he be young or old, it is never too late. G-d told the prophet Isaiah, "I will sweep aside your transgressions like a mist, and your sins like a cloud. Return to Me, for I will redeem you" (*ibid.*, 44:22).

We have a chance to rid ourselves of all sin and guilt, a chance to start a clean page. G-d has given us this opportunity. Do we dare neglect it?

TAKING TIME OUT

Modern society has been rightly described as a society of social climbers and status seekers. Keeping up with the Joneses isn't enough — everyone is busy trying to surpass them. We live in constant fear of being rejected by the right groups, and dread the horror of getting in with the wrong crowd. We want the world to know that we have arrived. We may not realize it, but more and more of our efforts go into surrounding ourselves with status symbols. We hope that these possessions will influence those who judge us, and we expect our material wealth to establish some social distance between ourselves and those we consider our inferiors. We must have a home in the right neighborhood, we must drive the right car, we must use the right charge cards, and we must belong to the right organizations. We are all under constant pressure to conform to this competition and we all suffer from its stress.

In order to be a successful social climber, one must be ready to make many sacrifices. He must discard his values and friends and be willing to change his behavior. Upon joining this social rat race, he may feel that his home address, or that of his club, may impede his progress. Even his house of worship may become a barrier, and so he changes his friends, his values, and his beliefs with each step up the ladder. Most certainly, he will find himself badly distressed and frightened by the unending process of social striving. He will find himself under constant financial strain as he tries to surround himself with visible evidence of the status he hopes to acquire. He will be constantly egged on by the mass media — television, newspaper and radio advertising, which single him out, taking advantage of his struggle to fulfill his ceaseless material aspirations.

In previous generations, this constant scramble for social success was virtually unknown. Each person knew his place in society and was content. If his father was a stonemason, then he too would be a stonemason. If his father was a farmer, then he too would till the soil. Today, each one of us wants to rise above the limitations of his father, and what was good enough for us as youngsters is certainly not good enough for our children.

All of this would be very admirable if it did not result in our committing sociological suicide. As we breathlessly claw beyond the social standing of our fathers, we often try our best to forget them entirely. We vainly try to disassociate ourselves from anything that could possibly remind us of them. We leave behind their old-world trappings, their traditions, their values, even their faith.

In a society devoted to grappling after material wealth, dedicated to the blind worship of Mamon, neither G-d nor faith seems to have much value. Religion becomes something of a joke. How wise was the prophet Moses when he predicted this age, when he prophesied just what would happen today:

> Jeshurun became fat and rebelled. You grew fat, thick and gross. (The nation) abandoned the G-d Who made it, and spurned the Mighty One Who was its support.... You thus ignored the Mighty One Who bore you; you forgot the Power Who delivered you.
> (Deuteronomy 32:15-18)

Moses went on to describe the terrible consequences of such behavior:

> I will heap evil upon them, striking them with My arrows. (They will be) bloated by famine, consumed

> by fever, cut down by bitter plague. I will send against them fanged beasts, with venomous creatures who crawl in the dust.
> (*ibid.*, 32:23-24)

Is such punishment inevitable? Can there be a cure for an entire society addicted to this mad clamor for status and wealth? Indeed there is. But rather than simply instructing us to abandon our lust for wealth, the Torah teaches us a better way. The Torah provides us with a better experience, the holiday of Succos. On Succos, we are commanded to stop, to interrupt our struggle for status and success, and to remember our humble beginnings:

> During (these) seven days you must live in thatched huts. Everyone included in Israel must live in such thatched huts. This is so that future generations will know that I had the Israelites live in huts when I brought them out of Egypt. I am G-d your L-rd.
> (Leviticus 23:42)

Even the one who lives in a vast mansion or on a palatial estate is commanded to forsake it all and to spend seven days in a Succah, in a small thatched hut. We are commanded to stop our endless social climbing with its flight from the past, and to remember our fathers who dwelt in simple huts in the wilderness. On Succos, we forgo our material strivings, to remember the L-rd our G-d.

There is a second major commandment on Succos, that of the four species:

> On the first day, you must take for yourself a fruit of the citron tree, an unopened palm frond, myrtle branches, and willows (that grow near) the brook. You shall rejoice before G-d for seven days.
> (*ibid.*, 23:40)

The Midrash gives us an interesting commentary about this mitzvah. It notes that each of these four species has a status of its own: the citron or *esrog* has both taste and fragrance; the palm branch or *lulav* gives forth taste but no fragrance; the myrtle has fragrance but no taste; and the willow has neither taste nor fragrance (*Vayikra Rabbah* 30).

So it is with humanity. There are some who are scholars, with the taste of learning, but they are apt to look down upon the ignorant, as being of no use to G-d or man. There are others who are wealthy, who have the fragrance of riches, who can support many religious institutions and do many good works. They are apt to feel that wealth is all that counts, that the person without money is without worth. If the scholar is so smart, "Why ain't he rich?"

But the Scripture tells us to take all four species, to bind them together to fulfill G-d's commandment. We must accept all people together, be they rich or poor, learned or ignorant. We must take the proud *esrog*, which has both taste and fragrance, both riches and learning, but we must also take the lowly willow, with neither taste nor fragrance, with nothing to show for itself, poor and ignorant. We must bind these all together to form a single brotherhood to serve G-d. As long as we leave out even one, we have not fulfilled our obligation.

Yet we are only too likely to overlook the poor and the ignorant. We live in a very stratified society. Many of our children have never met, much less spoken to, a child who has really known want. Quite to the contrary, we live in an age of unprecedented luxury, where all of our material wants are immediately satisfied, where we really have too much to eat, where children often have more spending money than did whole families of a generation ago.

We feel that this is a very admirable situation. This is the way things should be, and there is no danger lurking in all this plenty. But perhaps we should take a second look at our complacence.

A recent experiment performed by an Austrian ornithologist points a finger at this danger. Professor Otto Koenig of Vienna took a large colony of cattle egrets and housed them in a large enclosure where he could observe them. He allowed the birds to wallow in total luxury. With scarcely a move, they were able to get all the food that they could eat. There was plenty of water for drinking and bathing, and an endless supply of nest-building materials. The birds were given everything they needed — an existence of almost complete leisure.

Under normal conditions, these birds develop a society that parallels ours in many ways, including very strong feelings of family responsibility. But when they were subjected to a life of absolute ease, almost every pattern of family and group existence was disrupted. Care for the young was haphazard; at times, eggs were pushed from the nest and broken, and sometimes as many as three females tried to hatch the same brood. Normally, young egrets show a sturdy independence, but when they were raised in luxury and given an overabundance of leisure, they learned little about fending for themselves. Adult birds were still being fed like infants by their parents, or even grandparents. Young birds frequently pecked older ones to death, indulging in a form of cannibalism unknown under normal conditions.

Professor Koenig's experiments on birds can shed quite a bit of light on our own human problems. When we look at the many troubles that plague our youth — their insecurity, their lack of independence, the alarming rate of juvenile delinquency, drug addiction and sexual misconduct, even among our middle-class youth — and when we wonder what we have done wrong, we may find the answer in Professor Koenig's experiments. We may have produced a society that is strictly for the birds!

One of the foremost early American philosophers was Henry Thoreau. He wanted to prove to himself that man could escape the evils of the commercial world. In 1845 he went into the woods near Walden Pond where he lived alone for two years in an almost hermitlike existence. He built his home with his own hands at a cost of only $28.00. He fished, hunted and grew his own vegetables. He earned what little money he needed by doing odd jobs.

During his stay in the woods he kept a journal which he later published under the title *Walden*, one of the great classics of early American literature. Thoreau preached a return to nature with its innocence and simplicity; a return to a true system of values uncluttered by the clamor of the marketplace with its vain search for status and social standing; a return to a life divorced from the spurious values of the social climber.

The holiday of Succos is the Walden of the Bible. It calls us back to the simplicity and innocence of unadulterated nature. The Succah, the festival hut, is a many-splendored, colorful thing, yet no artificial color has been added. We are so accustomed to improve every thing we see, to paint and powder and touch up, that we seldom see the untouched beauty of nature — and we marvel at it.

The Succah reminds us that we can never improve upon the beauty of nature, no matter how much skill we have. The best we can do is approximate it. The Succah is built out in the open, frail and unprotected. It cannot even be built under the shelter of a tree. Yet it stands like a fortress, withstanding the forces of nature, and it brings gladness to the heart of man. It makes man thankful for the beauty of nature, lifting him up in prayer to G-d. The Succah is made of the stuff of the earth: all of its components grow in the dirt. Yet, by its sheer loveliness, it cleanses the heart of all pettiness.

It is perhaps significant that, today, Succos is one of our most neglected holidays. In a world of crass materialism there is no room for the G-dly, the spiritual, or even the naturally beautiful. There is little place for the faith of the past, for tradition, for holiness, or for truth. The poor Succah, therefore, stands abandoned and tattered, left to the mercy of the winds of change. Its once bright decorations have been torn down by grasping hands, its lovely fruits, devoured by greedy mouths. We are so busy running, how can we possibly find seven days to tarry in the Succah — or seven minutes, or even enough time to put our head in the Succah and utter a blessing? We are so busy, but do we know where we are going?

The festival of Succos is the time when we stop to seek direction, to see where we are running. We relax for a week by sitting in the Succah, returning to the simplicity of a dimly distant past and renewing our faith in the simple things of life. The Succah is waiting with its message of beauty and simplicity, beckoning us to enter, relax and tarry a while, to take some time out to enjoy life.

DUST FROM THE EARTH

The epic of creation, as told in the Torah, culminates in the formation of the first human being: "And the L-rd G-d formed man of dust from the earth, and He breathed in his nostrils a breath of life, and the man became a living soul" (Genesis 2:7).

Let us imagine ourselves transported back in time to the very origin of intelligent man. We can picture Adam opening his eyes, the first truly human act in the world. We can see him standing tall and bare on the red earth, his dark eyes full of wonder, glowing with a vast and perfect innocence. We can hear the first beating of his heart, feel the warm coursing of his blood, sense the strength of his arms and legs, the breath of air in his lungs. We can smell the sweet scents of the woods and flowers in his nostrils, see the wind ripple his hair, feel its coolness on his new skin.

We watch the expression on his face mirror the comprehension growing slowly in his mind. This sensing of a great Presence outside of himself increases as a spirit wells up within him. We watch in awe as he experiences sheer gratitude to this Presence before him, Who had formed him from the dust of the earth and had given him life.

With this first opening of his eyes, Adam emerged out of nothingness. One instant he was nonexistent, in the next he was a living soul, looking out on a new world and into the face of his Maker. In that unique moment of becoming a living soul, Adam could feel no fear. All the world was his garden, and the Creator had bid him welcome.

The Midrash tells us that Adam's first deed was to bless G-d. There were no questions in the heart of this first man, none of the puzzles that would plague his descendants. He had no need to ask, Where do I come from? Why am I here? Where do I go when I depart? Adam had no need to formulate these simple, yet profound, questions. The world was new and unknown, but Adam could sense the reassuring presence of G-d, and he felt at home.

All the world was Adam's domain. All was perfection, beauty, and comfort. His only restriction lay in the one commandment given to him by G-d: "You may eat freely of every tree in the garden, but of the Tree of Knowledge of Good and Evil you shall not eat, for on the day you eat from it, you shall surely die." Adam must have realized that the commandment was very simple, little more than a mere token of obedience to G-d who had given him his life. But G-d was putting Adam on his honor.

Then G-d created woman, Eve, as a companion for this first man. For a very short, blissful time, they lived in a true state of paradise in the Garden of Eden. But there was a snake in the garden; an unusual snake which stood on two legs and could talk. Exactly what this snake was, we do not know. Some say that the Evil One had entered the body of a serpent. A Midrash states that a serpent-like creature with the power of speech had been created especially to serve man.

Whatever this stranger was, his purpose was clear. He smiled at Eve. His voice was polite and had its own attractive music. He seemed genuinely interested in her well-being. But he was also quite impudent. "Is it true that you may not eat of any of the trees of the Garden?" Eve's expression revealed her amusement at such a silly question. Why, she could eat anything she wanted to! There was only one exception, and she told him so. The stranger smiled craftily. "Which one?"

Eve told him simply, without resentment, that they were forbidden to eat of the Tree of Knowledge, for to do so would be an act of disobedience to G-d, the One who had given them everything, including life itself. She added, "Surely I will die if I disobey G-d's commandment."

The stranger looked at Eve in disbelief. Such superstition! He threw back his head and just roared with laughter. How could one believe such a thing? The Midrash tells us that this "snake in the grass" took a large bite of the fruit, grinned at Eve, and said with a chuckle, "I ate the fruit! Look! G-d did not strike me dead! Most certainly you will not die!" The stranger leaned forward confidentially, and his voice fell to a whisper. How could it be that Eve did not understand why G-d had denied them this one thing? "The day you eat the fruit of this tree, your eyes will be opened. You shall be like G-d, knowing good and evil."

We all know how the story ended: "And Eve took from the fruit, and she ate, and she gave also to her husband with her, and he ate." But this story with its strange elements — a Garden of Eden, forbidden fruits, talking serpents — has a certain mystic air about it. In order to understand it, we must delve into the writings of the mystics.

One of the great Jewish mystics was the Chassidic leader, Rabbi Yaakov Yitzchak, who was known as the Chozeh, the Seer, of Lublin. The Chozeh paid careful attention to the wording of the passage in which the serpent said, "You shall be like G-d, knowing good and evil." Does one have to be like G-d to know good and evil? Didn't Adam and Eve understand these concepts before they ate from the tree? The truth is, both Adam and Eve certainly did have knowledge of good and evil when they were first created, but this knowledge was merely of an academic nature; they had not yet bridged the gap between theory and practice.

A person who reads and studies about something comes away with a certain amount of understanding. Someone who actually works with the subject has more intimate knowledge. And he, in turn, does not have the expertise of the one who discovered or invented it. For example, a man may spend years studying motors by poring over diagrams and reading manuals. He will understand the theories behind them, but he will never be able to fix a motor until he has had the kind of hands-on experience that a mechanic can boast. Even an expert mechanic will not have as much knowledge as the man who has designed and built a motor from scratch. It is for this reason that G-d has the most complete knowledge of all things. G-d created them, and He alone can fathom their full depth.

This is what the Evil One said to Eve: Now your knowledge of good and evil is merely academic. You have the knowledge of the student, not of the craftsman. You have learned about evil; you know that it is against G-d's will, but you have never created it. If you eat of the tree, then you will have G-d—like knowledge. Just as G-d knows the universe as its Creator, so will you know evil as its creator. Or, as the Midrash interprets this passage, just as G-d created His universe, you will create your own universe — of evil.

The serpent lied. Man's knowledge of good and evil can never equal that of G-d. G-d created good and evil as two very separate entities. It is in man that good and evil become confused. Not only does man justify his most hideous actions, he makes them appear as virtues. For example, Hitler labeled the murder of six million Jews the most noble deed in human history. We often find ourselves in an upside-down world, where the evil are praised as saints, and the good are damned as fiends.

G-d "makes peace and creates evil" (Isaiah 45:7). The evil that G-d created is actually the power He gave man which allows him to act as if G-d's omnipotence did not exist. With this power, man has absolute freedom of choice. He is free from both the tyranny of his nature and from obedience to G-d's will. If this were not the case, it would be utterly impossible for any person to commit a sin against G-d. "Behold, I have set before you this day, life and good as well as death and evil.... I call heaven and earth as witnesses... this day, that I have set before you life and death — the blessing and the curse

— but you shall choose life, in order that you may live, you and your children" (Deuteronomy 30:16-19).

In the Garden of Eden, G-d put Adam on his honor. In much the same way, we are on our honor. We must use our power wisely, and choose the right path, the path of the Tree of Life.

THE CALL OF THE SHOFAR

In ancient times, the shofar was used to assemble the people. In modern times, the shofar is used on Rosh Hashanah, a day when Jews all over the world assemble in their synagogues. Many who come may never set foot in a synagogue all year round, but when Rosh Hashanah draws near, it is as if there were a shofar in their hearts calling them to assemble, saying, "Return My children, return O Israel, unto the L-rd your G-d." The call is as loud and clear as a trumpet blast, and no Jew alive can turn away from it.

We blow a ram's horn to recall the great sacrifice that Abraham was willing to make, and the ram that he sacrificed in place of his son Isaac. The story appears in the 2nd chapter of the Book of Genesis. Its lesson is universal.

Let us imagine ourselves transported back in time almost 4000 years.* We see the patriarch Abraham trudging across a windy, fallow field in the land of Canaan. Suddenly, a great rapture, an unimaginable ecstasy, seizes him. He hears a voice that he has learned to trust and obey, the voice of G-d. It is the same voice that promised him a son in his old age; the same voice that promised that his children would be as numerous as the stars of the heaven. It is the voice that many years ago told him to leave his birthplace, to go forth from his father's house. It is a voice that has promised much, and has never failed to fulfill its trust.

---

* The following is based on the interpretation of *Ibn Ezrah,* as referred to by *Orach Chayim.*

On this windy afternoon, this voice comes to Abraham again, clearly, within the very depths of his soul. The voice calls his name, "Abraham! Abraham!"

The old man stands still in the wind-swept field. He looks around. Not a soul is in sight, but he recognizes the voice of G-d. Without hesitation, he exclaims, "Behold, here I am!"

Then he hears the voice again, stronger and more compelling. "Abraham! Take your son, your only son, the one that you love. Take Isaac and go to the land of Moriah. Take him to the mountain which I will show you, and there, offer him as a burnt offering."

Then the voice is gone. Only the howling of the evening wind seems to mock an old man standing in the gloom. Abraham stares straight ahead, his mind in a whirl. "O Voice of Almighty G-d, You cannot mean what I have just heard! My son? My Isaac? My dear beloved son, the joy of my old age, the promise of my future? The beloved son of laughter, Isaac, to be slaughtered like a beast on the altar, to have his dear flesh burnt as a sacrifice! Am I having a nightmare?"

As night falls, Abraham's thoughts begin to clear. He has been standing in the very place where he heard the voice. Now he begins to walk through the dusk. The command was no illusion. The Alm-ghty, the Creator, the One G-d, the True G-d, the Only G-d has spoken to his most obedient servant Abraham. The voice was unmistakable. The commandment was clear. Abraham has learned to love his son with a love deeper than the springs of the desert. Yet, as he walks through his fields, the silvery moonlight casting its eerie glow on the wheat and barley, Abraham asks himself, "Do I love G-d more than anything in the world, or do I love Isaac more than I love G-d?" The old Abraham is being tested as no mortal had ever been tested before or since.

All through the night Abraham tosses in his tent, a lonesome old man who is being asked to give up a son more dear to him than life itself. After a fretful night, Abraham knows that he can deny his G-d nothing. At the break of dawn he gets out of bed, and silently saddles his old white donkey. Without a word, he motions to two of his servants and to his son, his beloved son Isaac, to help him load a pile of wood onto the donkey. Then they set off in silence.

For three days they travel across the golden ripening plain of Mamre, on and on through the thickly wooded hills. All this time, Abraham walks in silence. He cannot bring himself to say a word to his son. His browned face is like a mask of stone, and the deep gleam in his eyes is like a fire burning in the depth of a cave. Finally, Abraham sees Mount Moriah from a distance. He tells his two servants to stay behind with the donkey. He loads the wood onto Isaac's strong young back. In his belt he carries flintstones for the fire, and hidden under his robe, a long straight knife.

The two walk together, father and son, alone among the foothills. Not a word passes between them. At last Isaac dares to break the silence, and says, "Father, it seems that we are going to worship and offer a sacrifice. We have the wood and the fire-stones, but where is the lamb for the offering?"

Abraham closes his eyes and holds back his tears. What can he tell his one and only beloved Isaac? He whispers, "G-d will provide the sacrifice, my son."

Isaac says nothing else, walking silently with his father. Never would the young man imagine that the very wood he is carrying is being taken to burn his own body, and that there is a special knife in his father's belt that is meant to cut his throat. Higher and higher they climb, until they finally reach a small plateau at the top of the mountain. Isaac watches as his father carefully gathers stones and piles them together to build an altar. He helps his father arrange the wood on the altar, and then his father motions to him to hold out his hands.

Before Isaac realizes what is happening, his wrists are tightly bound with strips of leather. His ankles are quickly bound also, yet not a word from the old man. Is his father playing some sort of game? He looks into his father's eyes for an answer and sees only tears. His father is quaking. Something is terribly wrong.

His earlier question comes back to him. Where is the lamb for the sacrifice? Suddenly, he knows. He himself is the lamb! His cheeks turn white, his eyes roll back in his head. He is a prisoner, bound fast beyond hope of escape. The old man gently lifts him onto the heap of wood piled on the altar. As if in slow motion he sees his father take a knife from beneath his robe and raise it to his throat. Isaac closes his eyes. He feels the cold metal against his skin, then everything goes blank.

Abraham holds the blade against his son's throat, hesitating, trying to summon up courage to finish the act. Suddenly, he hears the voice again, sounding like summer thunder, imperative and urgent. "Abraham! Abraham!"

He falters, puts down the knife, and answers, "Behold, here I am."

Stronger than ever, the voice returns. "Lay not your hand upon the lad. Do nothing to him, for now I know that you fear G-d, since you have not withheld your only son from Me."

Abraham hears no more. Through eyes blurred with tears, he sees a ram behind a pile of stones, caught by its horns in the bushes. The beast for the burnt offering has been waiting for him there. The test is over.

Our fathers learned from Abraham's example. No sacrifice was too great for them, either. Whatever was asked, whether it was to go to synagogue before a backbreaking day of work, or to go without food rather than eat something forbidden, or even to give generously while nursing an empty belly, they answered the call as did our forefather Abraham. "Behold, here I am, ready, without hesitation." In an almost forgotten day and age, the average Jew would attend the synagogue twice every day. In the bitter cold winter, he would slip out of his warm bed to face the freezing morning dawn, and go trudging through the snow to pray. Through the sultry heat of summer, supper would have to wait until the evening prayers were finished. Neither the heat of the day nor the cold of the night would keep even the most feeble and sickly Jew from his daily worship in the synagogue.

But today, the twice-a-day Jew has degenerated into a twice-a-year Jew. An article in *Time* magazine has shown that 78% of the Jewish people never see the inside of a synagogue except on the High Holidays. Daily worship is out of the question. Friday night services conflict with our cozy entertainment, whether a basketball game, a favorite television show, or dinner with an important client. Our fathers were willing to sacrifice their very lives for G-d, but apparently we are not willing to sacrifice even a small measure of our comfort.

Many Jews feel that they can buy their way into heaven by supporting Jewish causes. They are "alimony Jews," willing to support Judaism, but unwilling to live with it. Even this, however, can hardly be considered a sacrifice when you consider that over 13% of an average individual's income is spent on theater, sports and vacations; over 7% is spent on liquor, tobacco and candy, but less than 2% is spent on religion. That can hardly be called a sacrifice. Judaism expects much more.

In Jewish Law, there is a standard of giving that was unquestioned by our fathers. "If a person wishes to fulfill the precept of giving wholeheartedly, he should donate one-fifth of his income to worthy Jewish charities. The average person is required to give one-tenth of his net income. He who gives less than one-tenth is considered a miser" (*Shulchan Aruch, Yoreh Deah* 249:1). Buying one's way into heaven is not cheap. Does our level of giving come up to the expectations of our faith, or do we rely on good intentions, on a good Jewish heart?

Rabbi Abraham Kochev-Lev, the late leader of the Braslover Chassidic community in Jerusalem, once said that there is a place in heaven that is completely empty except for hooks, large golden hooks. Suspended from each hook is a palpitating human heart. The Rabbi explained that these are the "good Jewish hearts" that have found their way into heaven.

The real place for the good Jewish heart, however, is in the service of G-d through prayer. A good Jewish heart is a prayerful heart that longs to dwell in the house of the L-rd. For over 2500 years, the synagogue has been the center of all Jewish life, and the focal point of the Jewish community. The person who denies himself the synagogue is denying himself a constant source of spiritual nourishment and a vital part of his identity. He is also denying himself the brotherhood of the hundreds of generations that have made the synagogue their home. And he is denying himself a communion with G-d, the wellspring of all meaning in life.

Our grandparents and great-grandparents had a maxim: *"Es iz shver tzu zein a Yid* — It is difficult to be a Jew." But good things do not come easily, and that which comes too easily is often suspected of being worthless. True, it is hard to be a Jew, but one must recall the lesson of Abraham, to internalize the call of the shofar, and be prepared to sacrifice by giving of our time, effort, charity and love.

A CITY WITHOUT WALLS

One hears many theories about the causes of anti-Semitism, but one of the most interesting and novel theories is presented by the prominent Jewish writer, Maurice Samuel. He offers the following scenario:

A child says that he hates his Hebrew teacher. When asked why this is so, he is at a loss to explain it, even to himself. He may offer justifications and rationalizations for his feelings, but these prove to be merely excuses, and are obviously not the real reasons. When we examine his answers and try to understand his motivations, we find an astonishing truth. It is not the Hebrew teacher that he dislikes, but Hebrew school. The child loves to play football, and, if he could, would play every afternoon of the week. He cannot, however, because Hebrew school stands in his way. It is not the teacher that he resents, just his not being able to participate in the football games. In his subconscious the child transfers his resentment of Hebrew school to the person most immediately responsible for his missing the games, and he loudly proclaims that he hates his Hebrew teacher!

Maurice Samuel writes that this same transference of resentment may well be responsible for anti-Semitism. Two thousand years ago, only a small proportion of the people in the world were Jews; the vast majority were pagans. There is little question that it was far easier to be a pagan than to be a Jew. After all, there are a host of moral and ethical rules that are part and parcel of Judaism, and the pagan could ignore them all. But when the Christian religion was founded and the majority of the civilized people in the world became Christians, they could no longer ignore these ethical rules. They could no longer "play football" whenever they liked, because they now had a moral obligation to uphold. Just as the child in our example resented his Hebrew teacher because Hebrew school denied him the freedom to play football, so did the pagan subconsciously resent his moral teacher who denied him the free and easy life of the heathen.

The person who was responsible was Jesus, a Jew, whose teachings, which were later developed into Christianity, ultimately sprang from Jewish moral principles. The people, however, were afraid to blame Jesus openly. And so they transferred this resentment from him to encompass the entire Jewish nation.

A study of history will show that the Jews really annoyed their neighbors in ancient pagan times. They could not understand why the Jews would be revolted by their drunken binges and other forms of debauchery, especially when performed under the pretext of religion. Pagans often went to their temples not to worship or to pray, but to indulge in obscene orgies, and to offer themselves to their gods as an expression of religious adoration. Bacchus was nothing more than the god of drunkenness; Venus was the goddess of lust. The pagan ideal was well expressed by the Persian poet, Omar Khayyam, who wrote:

> To drink wine and make merry — such is my scheme of life;
> To pay not heed to heretic or devotee — such is my creed.

Today, this ideal is well on its way to becoming the creed of the masses. Depravity roams the streets of our big cities. In New York City, the municipal authorities had to enact an ordinance that nightclubs be closed before daybreak, so that the honest workers on their way to their tasks might not be outraged by the universal drunkenness and indecency that stalks unashamed in these modern shrines of Bacchus and Venus.

We know that no man sins without making excuses for himself. Before a person can conform to this society of shamelessness, he must have a philosophy of life that condones yielding to his every craving and that repudiates any summons to self-denial. Such a comfortable recommendation, however, is not altogether convincing to the true philosopher, to say nothing of the moralist, for the need for self-discipline needs no theological proof. A little knowledge of human nature will suffice.

Human nature is both good and bad. Somewhere in man's being is some primitive derangement that not only sets human nature against G-d, but even against his own best interests. Those who so confidently invoke the uninhibited philosophy of "psychology" often forget the primary psychological onset of guilt after having done something contrary to our own moral code. They leave the most important phenomenon in human history unexplained. They have no theory that can give a reason for the human sense of right and wrong.

Very often people speak of evolution and civilization, but somewhere they fail to recognize the true meaning of these words. If man were to always release his inhibitions, neither civilization nor evolution would be possible. According to the theory of evolution, man has been able to evolve, from a brutish individual to *Homo Sapiens,* by harnessing that which is animalistic in his nature. He has succeeded in becoming a true human being by emphasizing and cultivating those elements in his being that make him a man.

We need no Divine revelation to teach us this simple fact. It can be deduced from plain logic and common sense: If you let a beast have his way whenever he wants it, you shouldn't be surprised when he turns on you and tears you to pieces. It is no different with the animal cravings in man. If they are unrestrained, they will smother the spirit of man, and mankind will revert to paganism.

We may resent the yoke we bear, and we may feel discomfort

when we repress our beastly instincts, but civilization is surely worth the price. The harbingers of modern civilization that brought the concept of self-restraint to the world through their own example were our own ancestors. The Jew of old had a philosophy of life and a code of ethics that, coupled with an all-embracing spirit of Torah, gave their culture an ethos of self-discipline, even in the most prosaic enterprises. Sleeping, waking, washing, dressing and even the most basic bodily functions were all acts governed by Divine Law. "I have placed G-d before me at all times" was their motto. Life was lived in the presence of G-d.

The Talmud tells a remarkable story that illustrates this ideal. Rabbi Akiba, one of our greatest religious leaders, considered Rabbi Joshua to be a man of G-dly ways, a man from whom to learn. One evening, Rabbi Akiba hid under Rabbi Joshua's bed to see how he would get up, dress and wash in the morning. He later related this incident to his companion, Ben Azai. Ben Azai reprimanded Rabbi Akiba, asking him how he could do something so far beneath his dignity as a leader, something that showed such a lack of respect to the saintly Rabbi Joshua. Rabbi Akiba answered that all of man's actions were governed by Divine Law; that even such prosaic pursuits contained Torah wisdom, and he was determined to learn (*Brachos* 62a).

In the 13th century, when Rabbi Jacob ben Asher wrote his Four Pillars of Jewish Law, he called the first Pillar, the first book, *Orech Chaim*, The Way of Life. Judaism is more than a mere faith or philosophy. It is a continual code of self-discipline that comes not because of any external coercion, but from deep conviction.

A story is told about Rabbi Levi Yitzchak of Berditchev. Once the Czarist Russian government put a ban on the importation of all Turkish tobacco. Anyone found possessing this contraband would be severly punished. One day during Passover, Rabbi Levi Yitzchak asked his disciples for some Turkish tobacco for his pipe. They scattered through the ghetto and soon came back with several packets of tobacco, enough to fill a large can. Rabbi Levi Yitzchak then told his followers to bring him a piece of bread. They looked at him in astonishment and protested, "But Rabbi, it is Passover and we have no bread!"

The rabbi's face grew more stern. He repeated, "I command you as your Rabbi! Search the entire ghetto and bring me a piece of bread." His followers went all through the ghetto and ransacked every house in the ghetto. Several hours later they returned to Rabbi Levi Yitzchak and told him that they were sorry. They had fine-combed the entire ghetto, and they could not find a single crust of bread.

Then Rabbi Levi Yitzchak raised his eyes and said, "Master of the Universe, see how faithful Your children are. The Czar has hundreds of soldiers, police and agents guarding his borders, watching that no Turkish tobacco enter his land, yet in a short while, I can have all I want. But You, O G-d, have but once given Your children a commandment not to have bread in their houses on Pesach, and to this very day, not a scrap is to be found."

This concept of inner discipline was as incomprehensible to the ancient pagan as it is to the modern pagan, be he Jewish or otherwise. The ancient Greeks or Romans had no way of understanding the deep thirst for the Divine that kept alive this amazing self-discipline. They ridiculed the ancient Jews, but their value judgments were pretty dubious. The Romans might have nailed live people to wooden crosses in the name of justice, yet they recoiled in horror at the Jewish practice of circumcision. They pitted defenseless slaves against wild beasts for amusement, but they called the Jews barbaric for celebrating man's freedom from slavery on Passover. The ancient masters worked man and beast seven days a week mercilessly until they dropped from exhaustion, and looked with scorn upon our Sabbath which gave rest to all, freeman and slave alike. If a child was born with a face or nose that did not please its parents, the "graceful" Greeks would expose it to death, and they would laugh at the "graceless" Jews for recoiling at this custom. The ancient Jews did not look upon animal lust as the noblest form of human love. They placed duty to G-d above the pleasures of man. Because of this, the ancient Greeks and Romans looked down upon the Jews as barbarians.

So it is with the modern pagan. He spends his hours before the television as if it were the family idol, and he munches tranquilizers as if they were peanuts. Yet he looks with derision upon the self-disciplined, observant Jew and calls him a fanatic. But it is just this self-restraint that makes man a civilized human being.

"Like a city that is broken down and without walls, so is the man who has no control over his spirit" (Proverbs 25:28). To release man's inhibitions is to release his passions; and if we release all of man's passions then we shall destroy the human race. We shall cancel what little civilization we have; we shall lose what has been won by so many generations of discipline and self-denial. If we do as we please, in a century or two either we will be reduced to Hottentots and cannibals, or we will be blown off the face of the earth in a nuclear holocaust.

Throughout the ages, however, our teachers have realized that something else is required to make man perfect. After a person has subjected passion to reason, he must subject both passion and reason to G-d. It is only then that he can take his rightful place in creation. Man is no mere animal; he is not even merely a man. Man is a creation of G-d and he cannot be his whole self unless the rational conquers the animal, and both the rational and the animal acknowledge their allegiance to the Divine.

IS JUDAISM WORTH SAVING?

> And as for Me, this is My covenant with them, says the L-rd: My spirit that is over you, and My words that I have placed in your mouth, shall not depart from your mouth, nor from your children's mouth, nor from your grandchildren's mouth, says the L-rd, now or ever. (Isaiah 59:21).

Very often Jews express pride in being Jewish. "I'm proud to be a Jew" is a common catchword. I once heard about a rabbi who was a bit skeptical of this, and so he used an off-the-cuff "lie detector" test to determine whether people were sincere when they told him that they were proud to be Jewish. If, during the course of the conversation with the rabbi, a person would declare, "I'm Jewish, and I'm proud of it!" the rabbi had a standard reply. He would say, "I'm glad that you're proud to be Jewish, because you sure look Jewish!" The person would usually just look at the rabbi at first, to see if he were just kidding. When he realized that the rabbi was quite serious, his face would turn red from embarrassment, and he would emit a hollow laugh. He might have been proud to *be* Jewish. or at least he said he was, but he certainly wasn't very proud to *look* Jewish. This scenario took place time and time again.

If a person doesn't like the way he looks, he probably doesn't like the way he is. A man's physical self-image is a very revealing clue to his total self-image. The rabbi's little experiment seems to show that many Jews don't like themselves very much. No matter what they say, deep down they are really unhappy about being Jewish. And if this is the case, it raises a very legitimate question: Is Judaism worth saving?

Many Jewish young people are asking just that question. While the older generation asks whether Judaism will survive, the younger generation wonders whether it should. Is Judaism worth saving? Most of the barriers between the religions have been torn down; they see little difference between their Jewish friends and their non-Jewish friends. Many of our youth have abandoned Judaism without a qualm, and many marry outside of the faith without the slightest sense of guilt.

The problem becomes particularly acute in the area of intermarriage. Many young people, all very much in love, have asked me to marry them. When a mixed couple, a Jew and a Christian, approaches me, even though I understood what they are going through, I must answer them very sadly that I can not perform the ceremony. When they ask me why Judaism wouldn't recognize their love for each other, I tell them, honestly, that it is a matter of Jewish religious law. Judaism does not recognize the existence of marriage between a Jew and a non-Jew in any manner, shape or form.

Sometimes they persist. "What if we can get another rabbi to perform the ceremony?" they ask. I then tell them that all the ceremonies in the world could not legitimize such a union. Jewish law would look upon such a couple as not being married; they would be living in sin. When they ask me how Judaism could be so prejudiced, my only answer — the only answer — is that the Jewish people have always been a very small minority; if intermarriage were freely allowed, Judaism could not have maintained its identity and would have vanished long ago. Invariably, this couple that is so personally affected by my statement will ask me some very pointed questions: Is it desirable that Judaism exist as a separate entity, apart from the non-Jewish world? Would it not be better if we only had one world, one religion? If we really believe in the equality and brotherhood of all men, why should we be separated by religious barriers?

Answering these questions is really very difficult, because

though we understand them, we don't internalize them. These questions are not the result of our experience. Judaism has very strong emotional overtones for us, and we have a very big stake in Jewish survival. We still remember our grandparents; we have lived through the most tragic moments of Jewish history, and some of the most glorious. Moreover, Judaism has many lessons to teach in addition to those about G-d. Judaism has a history, a culture, and at least one language of interest. It has a homeland, institutions, and organizations. Judaism has a very strong ethnic dimension. Judaism can even be experienced in terms of emotion and nostalgia in an aesthetic dimension. In fact, there have been many writers who have had great success, or so it seems, in justifying Judaism without any theological basis at all. Therefore, our immediate answer is: Of course, Judaism should survive! Of course, Judaism is worth saving! We are surprised that the questions are even raised.

However, not all young Jews share these ties. Many are not interested in our emotional tribalism. They are looking for a logical answer that is meaningful to *them*, and relevent to *their* problems. We therefore must pose the question as a moral problem. Before we address the question, should Judaism survive, we must get our young people to focus on other related questions: Is Judaism good? Is Judaism worthwhile? Does it have something to offer the world? And even more important, does it still have something to offer the Jew? Only then can we ask what responsibility, if any, does a Jew have to preserve his faith.

It could be argued that Jews owe a debt to their past, and to the millions of martyrs who have given their lives for Judaism. How can one abandon a faith that so many people have given their lives to preserve? The emotional charge of this argument is so great that it is easy to lose sight of its logical weakness. Lives alone do not make a cause worthwhile. People have also given their lives for worthless causes, and even for evil causes. People gave their lives for Nazism, Communism, and to preserve slavery in the South. But none of us would consider these causes worth dying for, fighting for, or worth saving.

In examining the past, we find that Judaism's cause has so much to offer both the Jew and the world. Judaism gave the world the Bible and the "Judeo-Christian" ethic, producing the most successful culture on the face of the earth. But to insist that Judaism deserves to survive because of its past accomplishments is an invalid argument. Could an old man claim that he deserves to live forever because he accomplished much in his youth? In fact, many cultures have made great contributions to civilization and then have gone on to die. Should we revive and preserve them as well?

Some may argue that Judaism merits special consideration, since its contribution was unique. The Bible has given the world the most successful ethical system yet, not a museum artifact, but a vibrant part of world culture. Nonetheless, this too is not a valid argument for Jewish survival. After all, to benefit from the Bible, one doesn't even have to be Jewish!

Indeed, there are strong emotional arguments for Jewish survival, but logical arguments are much more elusive. We turn to our great thinkers and philosophers of old who surely have pondered this problem. While searching their vast writings for an answer, it is surprising to find that the question has never bothered the Jews. They firmly believed in G-d, and that G-d had a special mission for the Jews that would last for all time. Our sages didn't ask: Should Judaism survive? If G-d wanted it to survive, then it most certainly should survive. Belief in G-d and belief in Judaism have always been synonymous.

Yet herein lies the problem. Too many Jews do not have a very strong commitment to G-d. He is rarely taken into account in anything we do. One may say that he believes in G-d, but it is considered naive for a person to take G-d seriously in "practical" matters. Since Jewish survival is a very practical matter, it is felt that G-d should be left out of it. The theological dimensions of Judaism are precisely the ones that are taken least seriously.

But there is one thing that must be remembered. Judaism is rooted in a certain way of looking at the world. Take away this outlook, and in the cold light of objectivity, Judaism becomes meaningless. It is mere history, a relic, a museum piece. When you disallow the memories and the emotions, there is no logical reason for Judaism to exist. If Judaism is to be justified, it must include G-d. Without Him Judaism is just tribalism. If Judaism is worth saving, it must be a living Judaism with a philosophy for the world, firmly rooted in the G-d of Israel.

Not only does Judaism offer meaning for the present, it also offers a promise for the future, the Messianic promise made by a supernatural G-d, in a thoroughly supernatural manner. It is a promise that makes one's imagination soar, that makes the pulse beat a little faster, that makes Judaism the most meaningful idea extant. It is G-d's promise that the world will become a better place; war and strife, injustice and oppression will disappear. There will be a new world, and the Jew will be the maker of this new world. A great prophetic spirit, similar to the one under which the Bible was given, will return when all the Jews live in Israel in peace again.

Who is better qualified to teach the world Messianic ideals than the Jew? Who is better equipped to teach the world peace than the Jew, who did not have an army for over 1800 years? Who is better equipped to teach the world justice than the Jew, who has held Justice on the highest plane for his entire existence? Who is better equipped to teach the world brotherhood than the Jew, who actively preached brotherhood in an age where the equality of man was almost unknown? Who is better equipped to build a new world than the Jew, who has always preached that G-d will make a new and better world? A Judaism that is firmly rooted in the G-d of Israel has very much to teach the world.

The Talmud teaches us that there are three major periods of Jewish history. The first period, from Abraham until the destruction of the Second Temple in 70 C.E., is called the

Biblical period, the period when Judaism brought its great universal teachings to the fore. These teachings were then given to the world through Christianity and Islam. The second period was from the destruction of the Second Temple until the return of the Jews to Israel. This was the Talmudic period, the period where Judaism drew in upon itself and built up a great treasury of internal strength and ideology. Now we are approaching the third period, the Messianic era, when the Jew will again be in his own land, ready to proclaim his universal message to the world.

In the first stage, Judaism was a caterpillar, leisurely eating from the tree of life. In the second period, Judaism withdrew to the cocoon of self-realization. Now the butterfly is preparing to emerge, to soar to the loftiest heights, and to carry the rest of the world with it.

Is Judaism worth saving? No. Not as long as we feel compelled to ask the question. But with G-d's help, Judaism will exist. And in G-d's plan, Judaism must exist. And indeed, it will prove to be the most important thing that has happened in the world.

WAR RESISTANCE IN JEWISH LAW

The ethics of Jewish pacifism and war resistance has lately become a topic of intense discussion. However, most of these debates focus on general moral principles where Judaism has traditionally allowed a broad range of opinion. One can correctly argue that much of this is a matter of personal interpretation, and that war, under given circumstances, is just as defensible in Judaism as a pacifist position.

The only norm to which classical Judaism grants unequivocal authority is that of Halachah, Jewish religious law, where unambiguous statements and moral precedents can be cited. As in the case of secular law, the person rendering a decision still has considerable latitude in applying the law to a particular case, but the findings of a halachic authority do have the force of a basic teaching of Judaism.

The main halachic question involved in any discussion of war is the issue of the taking of human life. Judaism forbids killing in the very strongest terms, counting murder as the worst possible of sins. The murderer is listed among those eternally damned, as the Scripture alludes, "A man who is laden with the blood of any person shall hasten his steps into hell and none will support him" (Proverbs 28:17). The Talmud goes so far as to state that the main reason the story of Adam is included in the Torah is to teach us that humanity began with a single life, and therefore, the taking of even a single life is equivalent to destroying an entire world.

Murder is one of the three cardinal sins which may not be violated, even to save a life, the other two being idolatry and incest. Maimonides writes, that of the three cardinal sins, murder is the worst, since it is a wrong for which one can never ask forgiveness of the person wronged. So great is the sin of taking an innocent life that one may not kill a single human being even to save the lives of an entire community.

There are four cases, however, where Halachah does allow the taking of human life. These include self-defense, defense of an innocent life, penalties imposed by the courts, and war.

Even though Judaism teaches that one may not kill one innocent person to save another, this rule does not apply in the case of self-defense. As soon as a person attacks another, he is legally considered an assailant, and since he is no longer an "innocent person," he may be killed in self-defense. The Talmud accordingly teaches us, "If one comes to kill you, rise up and kill him first."

Just as Halachah allows killing in self-defense, so does it require a person to use any means necessary to prevent the murder of an innocent person, even if it involves killing the assailant. Killing is absolutely a last resort, however, and is only permitted when all other means have either been exhausted or ruled out as impossible. Even then, it is nothing less than murder.

The third instance when the taking of human life is permitted is in carrying out the death penalties prescribed by the Torah for the courts to execute. This was restricted to courts designated by the Sanhedrin, the supreme court and legislature of the Jewish people. However, capital punishment was abolished by Jewish courts in the year 30 C.E., and since that time, no religious body has had the right to decide in any life and death case. Even when in force, these penalties were considered primarily "book laws" designed to dissuade would-be offenders. In practice, they were hardly ever invoked. Indeed, the Talmud tells us that any court that invoked the death penalty as often as once in seventy years was considered bloodthirsty. Finally, when the number of offenders increased so much that the death penalty became inevitable, it was abolished completely.

Another factor mitigating the existence of a death penalty in Judaism was the strictness of the rules of evidence for capital cases, which made it virtually impossible for the courts to reach a guilty verdict. Indeed, some Talmudic authorities were in favor of making the rules of evidence so stringent as to effectively abolish the death penalty completely. As a further mitigating factor, death penalties were not administered by professional executioners, but by the principle witnesses in the case, thereby dissuading them from testifying unless the evidence overwhelmingly demanded such punishment.

The final instance in which killing is permitted is in time of war. However, it is most important to carefully distinguish between war and corporate or mutual defense. The Halachah regarding corporate defense is merely an extension of that regarding individual defense: Just as an individual may kill his assailant in self-defense, so may the inhabitants of a city or nation fight and kill the members of an attacking force in order to save their own lives. Likewise, citizens of a third city or nation may fight and kill members of an attacking force in order to save the lives of the beleaguered populace. In such cases, each individual member of the attacking army is considered to be an assailant, and may be killed in the same manner as a person attacking an individual.

War is an entirely different situation. In the case of war, members of the enemy army are killed even when they are not actively engaged in attack. Whereas in corporate defense, only such force as is absolutely necessary to save life may be used, war involves violence far beyond this measure. In corporate defense, one may not punish the assailant after subduing him, nor take revenge against his person, family, or property, nor use any unnecessary violence against him, his territory, or his community. In war, however, an entirely different standard exists wherein one group is labeled as the enemy, and within the regulations of war, any force or violence may be used against this group in order to subdue it and coerce it to surrender.

Historically, Judaism seems to have condoned and even encouraged war. Classical Judaism speaks of two types of war: *Milchemet R'shut*, permitted war, and *Milchemet Mitzvah*, compulsory war. It is important to note, however, that one of the foremost halachic authorities, Rabbi Ezekiel Landau, writes that conditions do not exist today that would in any way permit either of these two types of war. Nevertheless, these two types of war merit careful study. Compulsory war basically includes the two wars prescribed in the Torah, namely the war against Amalek, and the war of conquest when the Israelites entered Canaan. Both of these wars were counted as religious obligations of the Jewish people as a whole, and were numbered among the 613 commandments of the Torah.

Because of the existence of a Divine commandment to wage war, many people have concluded that Judaism teaches that war and revenge are virtues, and that religious, or holy wars, are condoned by the Torah. At first glance, this claim seems to be well-supported, and indeed, both of these commandments seem patently genocidal in nature. Regarding the war against the Canaanite aborigines, the Torah states, "When the L-rd your G-d delivers them into your power and you defeat them, you must utterly destroy them — you shall not make any treaty with them nor show them mercy" (Deuteronomy 7:2). Similarly, regarding Amalek, we find, "When the L-rd your G-d gives you peace from all the enemies around you in the land which He is giving you, then you shall blot out the memory of Amalek from under the heaven — you shall not forget" (*ibid.*, 25:19). These commandments, however, are not as genocidal as they might first appear, since they are mitigated by a third commandment: "When you advance upon a city to attack it, you shall first make them an offer of peace. If the city accepts this offer of peace and opens its gates to you, then all its inhabitants shall surrender and be subjugated by you" (*ibid.*, 20:10,11). According to the majority of halachic authorities, this commandment even applies to the war against

Amalek and the Canaanites, and therefore, even these enemies have the option of seeking peace and surrendering. Thus, these wars were not genocidal in nature, and as Nachmanides indicates on the basis of numerous Biblical sources, these nations actually were never destroyed.

The very existence of Divine commandments to wage war raises another important point. Where war and human lives are concerned, human judgement alone is not to be trusted; the decision regarding these preemptive wars must be based upon a Divine commandment. The very fact that the Torah mandates such wars indicates that it considers them to be of overriding historical importance to the very survival of the Jewish people and to civilization as a whole (Deuteronomy 7:4). The very Law that commanded us not to kill, harm our fellow, nor take revenge, was the same Law that ordained these wars. These two cases were unique exceptions to the rule that war is both sinful and forbidden, and therefore, they do not imply that the Torah condones or encourages war in any way. Finally, the concept of religious or holy war has gone against the very grain of Jewish teachings throughout our entire history.

The third category of compulsive war is the war of self-defense. Such war, however, is in reality corporate self-defense, as Rabbi Yehudah Gershoni indicates, and therefore its rules follow those of individual defense rather than those of war. The main reason that self-defensive war is categorized along with compulsory and permitted war is because it can be waged without consulting the Sanhedrin, as can wars involving Amalek and the Canaanites. It is in this point that we find the main difference between compulsory and permitted war. A permitted war could only be fought if condoned by the Sanhedrin, whereas compulsory war was ordained by the Torah itself and required no further authority.

The Sanhedrin was a body of seventy religious leaders whose authority to interpret and legislate religious and moral law is prescribed by the Torah itself. In its interpretive authority, it was the religious equivalent of our Supreme Court whose interpretation of the Constitution, no matter how farfetched, is legally the law of the land. The legislative authority of the Sanhedrin gave it the power not only to legislate in all areas of law, but also to temporarily abrogate any religious or moral law.

It was this final power which enabled the Sanhedrin — and only the Sanhedrin — to declare a war that was not specifically ordained by the Torah. War is inherently forbidden by religious law. Therefore, it could only be waged when this law was temporarily suspended by the Sanhedrin. In declaring war, the Sanhedrin had to temporarily suspend many commandments, including those forbidding murder, injury, and the destruction of property. Nevertheless, even when war is declared, the Torah requires that every effort be made to prevent loss of life, even that of the enemy. First, every means of peaceful negotiation must be explored. Secondly, it is forbidden to completely surround an enemy, thereby allowing an avenue of escape. Thus, even when war is permitted, killing is allowed only when no other alternative exists.

Since the final decision regarding war rests exclusively with the Sanhedrin, the religious and moral authority of the Jewish people, permission to wage war is granted solely on the basis of moral and ethical principles. However, since the Sanhedrin has ceased to exist, no corporate body within Judaism has the authority to condone or permit war.

All of this suggests that a Jew is forbidden to fight in any war today. The only possible exception would be a case of obvious corporate self-defense. A Jew is therefore by definition a conscientious objector, that is, one who is forbidden to fight and kill on the basis of his religious beliefs.

This is supported by historic precedent. The Jews are the only group in existence who have gone as long as 1800 years without any armed force of any kind, and for much of this period, most of its members simply never bore arms. The pacifist tradition in Judaism was patent in times of persecution and pogrom, when the Jew traditionally abstained from violence, even in self-defense.

There are some would-be authorities who claim that one has a duty to obey the law of the land, even if it requires him to fight and kill. Usually, this argument is based upon the Talmudic edict, *Dina DeMalchuta Dina* — The law of the government is law. However, both the Talmudic context of this rule and the opinion of the majority of commentators indicate that this statement merely means that legal forms instituted by the secular government are recognized by Jewish law. Furthermore, halachists are careful to point out that there is no obligation to obey civil law when it actually opposes religious law. Quite to the contrary, Judaism requires us to actively oppose any government edict requiring us to violate any religious law, no matter how trivial, and we are required to place our lives on the line, if necessary, in such a case. This is particularly true with regard to killing, even in war, since religious law requires that one give his life rather than kill.

There is another closely related point that bears consideration. If any rabbi were to decide that a person is duty bound to fight for his country, then that rabbi would be rendering a decision that may result in another person being killed. And as another important principle states, *Ain danin diney nafashot ba'zman ha'zeh* — No present-day authority has the right to judge a case where human life is involved. As Rabbi Joel Teitelbaum writes, one who renders a decision resulting in the loss of a single human life is guilty of murder (*Kuntres Al HaGeulah VeAl HaTemurah*, No. 44, p. 85).

Some argue that the prohibition against taking life does not apply in war, since every soldier on the battlefield is actually fighting in self-defense. However, another halachic concept is involved here. A person who has an opportunity to avoid a predicament where he may be forced to sin, and does not take advantage of this oportunity, bears full responsibility for his actions, even though he was forced to sin at the time. If one could have avoided being on the battlefield in the first place, the fact that his life is endangered does not exempt him from the moral responsibility of killing.

Even if one were to resolve not to kill, it would still be forbidden to appear on the battlefield. One's very presence is, in effect, provoking the enemy to attack and kill; in provoking another to sin, one is morally responsible for his act. We find an interesting precedent for this in the Talmud, where we are taught that it is forbidden for a father to strike his grown son, since it is likely to provoke the son to retaliate and violate the honor and respect due a parent. A father who violates this rule is guilty of violating the commandment "Do not place a stumbling block before the blind" (Leviticus 19:14), which, according to tradition, refers primarily to the morally blind. The same would be true of a person who provokes an enemy soldier by his appearance on the field of battle. Furthermore, he would be included in the dread malediction, "Cursed is he who makes the blind go astray in his way" (Deuteronomy 27:18).

The same commandment also forbids one to be an accomplice to any sin. Talmudic law teaches us that one who causes another to sin shares legal responsibility for the act, and therefore, it is forbidden even to give verbal encouragement to any person doing wrong. Thus, where war is forbidden, one is required to withhold any and all support of the war effort.

The Torah, however, requires much more than mere passive nonsupport of wrong. There is a commandment to speak up and protest any wrong, based on the Scripture, "You shall surely rebuke your people, and so not bear their sin" (Leviticus 19:17). Furthermore, where human lives are involved, one who does not do everything in his power to prevent death is guilty of violating the commandment, "Stand not idly by the blood of your fellow man" (*ibid.*, 19:16). One who does not make every attempt to prevent moral wrong is also included in the Biblical malediction, "Cursed is the man who does not uphold all the words of this law" (Deuteronomy 27:26). Even where it appears futile, one is still required to protest, as the Prophet Ezekiel was told, "If you do not warn the wicked to give up his evil ways and so save his life, the guilt is his; he shall die because of his evil, but G-d will require his blood from your hand. But if you have warned him, and he still continues in his wicked and evil ways, then he shall still die because of his evil, but you have saved your own soul" (Ezekiel 3:18-19). In our context, all of these commandments would require one to protest, speak out and demonstrate against war and killing in any form.

We therefore see that a careful study of Halachah, Jewish religious law, unambiguously indicates that war is forbidden, and that killing, even in war, is nothing less than murder. The only possible exception is corporate defense, but even then, any killing that is not absolutely necessary is considered to be murder. Furthermore, war may not be supported in word or deed, and must be protested to the fullest extent.

THE GENERATION GAP

> Behold, I will send you Elijah the prophet before the coming of the great and terrible day of the L-rd. And he will turn the heart of the fathers to the children, and the heart of the children to their fathers, lest I come and smite the land with utter destruction. (Malachi 3:23-24).

Much is said about the generation gap, about teenagers and college students who no longer communicate with their parents, about parents who have lost contact with their children. The generation gap is not a new phenomenon. Socrates spoke about it 2,400 years ago and the theme is repeated throughout history. The reason for this is only too apparent: a sixteen- or twenty-year-old does not see things in the same way a forty- or fifty-year-old does. The two have different ideals and problems. There will always be a generation gap.

Until now, generation gaps did not have serious consequences, because children grew up in an environment much like that of their parents. As they matured, they found that they regenerated their parents' values. The generation gap did not present a major problem because there was no regeneration gap. Today, the situation is different. The environment in which our children are growing up is almost totally different from that of their parents. The parent generation of today grew up in a world that knew nothing of such commonplace things as television, jet planes, nuclear bombs, lasers, computers, impersonalized I.D. numbers or human rights movements. Young people today are exposed to the mass media to an extent never before equalled in history. They are strongly influenced by social currents such as the "new morality" and the drug subculture. The two worlds are so different that our youth find it next to impossible to regenerate their parents' values. We are not faced with a generation gap, but rather a regeneration gap.

This problem is particularly acute for Jewish families in which the parents have not been successful in communicating Jewish values to their offspring. When such parents implore their children to live up to Jewish teachings, they find themselves speaking to a blank wall. Where did the parents fail? They failed when they urged their children to spend six hours a week in Hebrew school, but were themselves too lazy to spend an hour in the synagogue. In essence, they said, "Do as we say, not as we do." They showed by their actions that Judaism is only for children, not adults. When religion is not taken seriously by parents, it leaves the children without the strength and support that our great faith can provide. They find themselves walking a tightrope, when Judaism is actually a broad, smooth road.

An individual growing up today faces an array of serious problems, and is constantly faced with new opportunities for independence and responsibility which challenge his or her maturity. While looking for guidance, he or she may develop many close relationships; some may be wonderful, while others may turn out to be harmful. Sometimes, difficult decisions have to be made that may mean going against the crowd. Judaism can give a young person the self-assurance needed to withstand the peer pressures that he or she will inevitably encounter. Judaism's firm standards of conduct, which are based on keen insights into human behavior, and its profound answers to life's questions will help young people face the challenges of modern society.

Young people have a great disdain for sham in any form; they are quick to puncture cliches and platitudes in any and every variety. At the same time, they have a refreshing openness to new ideas, and face the world with a corresponding honesty.

They want to know things as they are and say it as it is. They find great joy in life, and they have a great ability to express it.

Our youth have the potential to regenerate a Judaism that is more meaningful and honest than anything that their parents may have ever experienced. We live in a world where people are searching for identity. If our young people can bridge the regeneration gap, they will find themselves as Jews. When they find themselves as Jews, they will also find themselves as human beings. We look forward to the day when this will happen, for it will be a day when Judaism will become something that we can hardly imagine in our fondest dreams.

THE END OF DEATH

We stand today on a fantastic threshold of scientific discovery. It seems that man himself is becoming the master of life and death. Consider the medical miracles that enable the transplant of healthy organs of mortally wounded people into the bodies of persons who would be otherwise doomed to die of incurable diseases. At Stanford University, biochemists have succeeded in synthesizing an active virus, a major step that could lead to the creation of life itself.

These are truly fantastic concepts, yet have we ever taken the time to consider their moral, religious and prophetic implications?

Let us start by thinking back to the Israeli Six Day War. From a practical, mundane standpoint, it was a minor war. From a theological standpoint, however, it had tremendous, universal impact because, for the first time in 2000 years, Jerusalem returned to Jewish hands. This is a simple fact, but one that has very far-reaching inferences.

Until that summer, the many prophecies in the Bible, Talmud and Midrash that relate to the coming of the Messianic age were nebulous statements referring to a distant future, having no direct bearing on our lives. We lived in the age of promise. Beginning in that summer, however, the age of promise passed and the age of fulfillment began. The first prophecy beginning to be fulfilled was the restoration of Jerusalem to the Jewish people. Now we can expect others to approach fulfillment.

One of the important prophecies regarding the Messianic age is the conquest of Death. Death will be vanquished, or, as Scripture says, "He will swallow up death forever, and the L-rd

G-d will wipe away tears from all faces." One hundred years ago people laughed at such prophecies as being impossible and ridiculous. Today, people no longer laugh; they merely look at the headlines.

The first steps toward immortality have already been taken. We can now transplant hearts, kidneys and livers. There are now techniques to clean out hardened arteries. Prosthetic devices, such as artificial hearts and artificial kidneys, can and will give many people a new lease on life. Doctors can literally give new life to previously hopeless patients. Furthermore, we must remember that most of these techniques are only several years old. We are still in the Model T stage, or perhaps the horse and buggy stage, of these techniques. We can only guess at what will be possible a mere ten or twenty years from now.

One of the exciting possibilities that is being seriously discussed is a brain transplant. It has already been done successfully with animals. This would result in a very interesting sort of immortality: No matter how badly damaged the body is, as long as the brain is unimpaired it could be transplanted into a healthy body, and the owner of the brain would live on. The brain of an eighty-year-old man could be transplanted into the body of a twenty-year-old, thus giving him an additional sixty years of life.

The only problem involved in a brain transplant is finding a donor. I imagine many people would not be willing to donate their body, no matter how worthy the cause. But another option presents itself. A person *can* donate his own body to himself.

As mentioned, biochemists have succeeded in synthesizing an active virus. Taken several steps further, scientists may be able to duplicate living cells. Each cell in a person's body contains the master plan for his entire being. This information is locked up in the genes and chromosomes and DNA molecules. With advanced techniques, it should be possible to take a single cell from an aged or broken body and grow it into a complete young and healthy body. (What is really amazing is the fact that such a process was described in detail in a Midrash written almost 2000 years ago!) A person's brain could then be transplanted into this new body which he, himself, provided!

Looking even further into the future, it is not at all inconceivable that drugs may be developed that could halt, or even reverse, the process of aging. As we learn and understand more about life, we can learn to control this process. After all, aging is nothing more than a chemical reaction, and many chemical reactions can often be stopped or reversed.

Imagine a world of immortals, a world without death. Such a society would be as different from ours as our civilization is from that of the caveman. Yet, such a world may be only twenty or thirty years away!

Immortality could help many people find greater fulfillment in life. Picture, if you will, a sixty-year-old who yearned to be a doctor. Today, such a dream would remain exactly that, a dream. He would simply not have enough years left to him to make such an investment in time worthwhile. But what about an immortal?

Consider war in a world without death. It is often said that old men start wars, and young men die in them. An old man has his life behind him; he does not have very much to risk in a war. Would that same "old" man react differently if he had many more years to which he could look forward? Will an immortal risk losing centuries of life in a nuclear war? It may well be that such a world will be the spark, the beginning of Isaiah's prophecy, that "nation shall not lift up sword against nation, neither will they learn war anymore."

Consider the importance of morality to a population of immortals. The prophet says that the creed of the hedonist is, "Let us eat and drink, for tomorrow we shall die" (Isaiah 2:13). But what if we shall not die tomorrow? We rush to satisfy our passions out of fear that if we do not satisfy them now, soon we will be too old to enjoy them, or soon we may die. If we no longer have this fear, perhaps we will tire of transient pleasures after two or three hundred years of life, and, instead, seek the Eternal.

To many of us, this all may seem strange. If we think of the Messiah at all, we think of him as some magical being coming out of the sky surrounded by clouds of glory. We imagine that the fulfillment of the Messianic prophecies will be miraculous and sudden, the way a magician pulls a rabbit out of a hat. This is a result of our thinking pattern which separates the practical world into one category and religious teachings into another. But this is false thinking. The Midrash states that the Messianic promise will come gradually, like the rising of the sun.

One of the most important lessons that we must remember is that there is nothing wrong, immoral, or unnatural about medical immortality. Immortality is merely one of our Messianic prophecies: "He will swallow death forever." The era of fulfillment has already begun!

WHEN BONES RISE AGAIN

The hand of the L-rd was upon me, and He carried me out by His spirit, and He put me down in a valley full of bones. He made me pass all around them, and there were very many bones in the open valley, and they were very dry. And He said to me, "Man, can these bones live again?" And I said, "Only You know that, G-d." And G-d said to me, "Prophesy over these bones, and say to them: Dry Bones, hear the word of G-d. This is G-d's word to these bones. I will put a spirit into you, and you shall live. I will fasten sinews onto you, bring flesh onto you, cover you with skin, and put breath into you, and you shall live; and you shall know that I am G-d."

I began to prophesy as G-d told me, and as I prophesied, there was a loud rattling sound, and the bones fitted themselves together. And as I looked, sinews appeared on them, flesh covered them, and they were covered with skin, but there was no life in them.

And G-d said to me, "Prophesy to the spirit, man, and say to it: These are G-d's words. Come spirit, from every direction, and enter these corpses, so that they may come to life."

I began to prophesy as G-d had told me, and a spirit entered them, and they rose to their feet — a very large army.

Then G-d said to me, "Man, these bones are the whole people of Israel. They say, 'Our bones are dry and our hope is gone. The final decree has been set against us.' Therefore, prophesy and say to them: These are the words of G-d: My people, I will open your graves, and bring you up from them, and I will return you to the land of Israel. You shall know that I am G-d, when I open your graves, and raise you up from them, and let you live in your own land. Then you shall know that I am G-d, and I will do as I have spoken. This is the very word of G-d."

(Ezekiel 37:1-14)

This amazing story, told by the prophet Ezekiel, prefaces a little-known but fundamental belief of Judaism, the last of Maimonides' thirteen principles of faith: "I believe in perfect faith that there will be a resurrection of the dead at the time that G-d so chooses."

This principle has very important theological implications. One of the foundations of all religion is the belief in G-d's ultimate justice. Unless we were to believe that there is some private reward and punishment of which we are not aware, we could question why the wicked prosper and good people suffer. We believe, however, that there is another judgment that occurs after death.

Usually we think of immortality as a state of everlasting bliss for the soul. But since the human body is very much an integral part of man, it is very difficult to imagine how a disembodied soul can in any way function as a true human being. The basic teachings of Judaism eliminate this question, while recognizing its implications.

Judaism teaches that the separation of body and soul is temporary. Man's ultimate reward will come with the resurrection in the World-to-Come, during the Messianic age. The dead will literally be brought to life, complete with the memories of both their former lives and this period of separation. They will then live again in this new world, a perfected world.

Many feel that this is the most farfetched of all Jewish beliefs. Patently, it involves a miracle of the highest degree. Assuming that dry bones can be brought to life, what about people who were eaten by wild animals, or blown to bits by an explosion, or vaporized at Hiroshima?

I think that the key to the entire question is found in a Midrash dealing with a controversy between the two major schools of Judaism of the time, Bais Shammai and Bais Hillel. Bais Shammai says that the resurrection will be a patent miracle in which G-d will bring life back to whatever human remains exist. Bais Hillel's thinking differs considerably. The resurrection will be a natural process, paralleling birth. The resurrected person will begin as a single cell, developing into an embryo, then a fetus, and then continue to grow into a full human being (*Berashis Rabba* 14). Bais Hillel bases its opinion on a very interesting passage in the Book of Job, which speaks about man's fate. Job says to G-d:

> Remember now, You formed me like clay, and You shall return me to the dust. But You will pour me out like milk, and curdle me like cheese, and clothe me with skin and flesh, and knit me together with bones and sinews. You have granted me life and continuing favor, and Your providence shall continue to watch over my spirit (Job 10:9-12).

There are two additional important factors in Jewish tradition regarding the resurrection. One is the tradition of the Luz, a bone of some sort, or as it is called in the Bible, the key to the resurrection. The other is the tradition of a "dew of resurrection," which is alluded to by the Prophet Isaiah:

> But Your dead shall live, their bodies will rise again. They that sleep in the earth will awake and shout for joy, for Your dew is a dew of sparking light, and

with it, the earth will bring those long dead to birth again.
(Isaiah 26:19)

The *Zohar* combines both of these traditions. The Luz, one for each person, will be placed in the dew of resurrection, and it will grow into the body of that particular person.

Finally, both the Mishnah and the Talmud suggest that good people will receive Divine inspiration to bring the dead back to life (*Sotah* 9:15; *Pesachim* 68a).

These allusions to the mechanics of the resurrection can be understood scientifically. G-d will reveal the genetic code required for duplication to a Divinely inspired group of peoples, who will place the Luz containing the RNA into the "dew of resurrection," a nutrient fluid. Under the right conditions, an exact duplicate of any human body could be grown.

The final stage of the process will be completed by G-d when He restores the soul to the body. This will be the true miracle of Resurrection.

When we examine our traditions carefully, the concept of resurrection is not as farfetched as it seems. The world of the resurrection will be a world where death is not only conquered, but where death can be reversed; it will be a world very different from the one we know now. It is the world our traditions speak of: the world of the Messianic Era, the world of our final hopes.